My Own True Story

The Journey of a Real Estate Appraiser

Mel H. Castelin

With Foreword by Raymond Aaron, New York Times Bestselling Author

Published by
10-10-10 Program
Markham, Ontario
CANADA

Table of Contents

DEDICATION

I owe my deepest appreciation to my mother who made numerous personal sacrifices and showed unconditional love. So I dedicate this book to her.

ACKNOWLEDGEMENTS

Although I have dreamed of writing a book for quite a while, it was a presentation in 2015 by Raymond Aaron that got me started writing this book. My sincere appreciation goes to Raymond Aaron.

My many years of research, in the real estate appraisal field, resulted in a wealth of information being collected about real estate and various individuals in the industry. In addition, my curiosity and desire to read many books uncovered some startling information which has been outlined herein.

Certain information contained in this book has been referenced throughout as footnotes. But the list of books which have been my reading material over the past several years, and have provided much of my critical thinking, are too numerous to mention herein. Many of the authors and speakers are featured in the alternative news media and they have a growing number of followers.

FOREWORD

I am delighted to have this opportunity to introduce you to Mel Castelin's book, *My Own True Story*, which relates some interesting events in the life of a real estate appraiser and the time he has spent dealing with some injustices. The book will open a path for you that avoids pitfalls.

The book also addresses a number of important issues which concern all of us. In addition to reading about the type of work done by an appraiser, you will learn that one can encounter all sorts of issues in workplaces, and regarding legal issues in real estate.

My Own True Story highlights some critical events, caused by certain corporations, which have resulted in serious damages. Mel indicates that in order for this world to be a better place, there should be no wars, violence, shooting of innocent people, illegal drugs, organized crime, human trafficking, corrupt politicians, cigarettes, harmful food additives, chemicals in our drinking water, pollution of our environment –or politicians who are controlled by lobbyists, donors, and special interests, to the detriment of the public.

Reading this inspiring book should encourage you to allow yourself to find solid values in order to guide your life and assist in making this world a better place. The value of relationships, caring, and doing the right thing, are needed in both relationships and businesses, and *My Own True Story* shows that, without them, businesses are destined for failure in the long run.

Reading this inspiring book should not result in apathy but trigger a call to action where politicians and other leaders in business are held accountable, so that beneficial change materializes.

Raymond Aaron
New York Times Bestselling Author

INTRODUCTION

My desire to write a book has been in existence for quite a while, but the thought was shelved by me as my work kept me fully occupied. The purpose of this book is to relate the life of a real estate appraiser, and also tell about some of my personal experiences and certain major issues of importance, which I have been wanting to express for quite some time.

The real property market is a key building block of the Canadian economy and affects every segment of our society. I was an accredited real estate appraiser and belonged to the Appraisal Institute of Canada (AIC). Real estate appraisal professionals play a direct and vital role in the real estate sector. That role is to determine, report upon, and attest to the real value of property. Their valuation is the foundation upon which informed decisions about real estate are made – whether by a family purchasing their first home, a farmer selling a piece of acreage, a retailer deciding where to locate his next outlet, a developer considering a vacant site, or a lawyer defending or prosecuting a case. AIC-designated appraisers are trained to complete appraisal, review, consulting, and reserve fund planning assignments within their area of competence.

Since I was 21 years of age, my work as a real estate appraiser involved inspecting various types of properties and preparing reports. During a period of 40 years, I worked for the provincial government, crown corporation, municipal government, and a private firm which necessitated extensive travel on appraisal assignments in Northern, Southwestern, and

Eastern Ontario. During my initial working years, I was too preoccupied with studying and working, and was unaware of the intricacies of large organizations. What Benjamin Disraeli said comes to my mind, namely: "The world is governed by very different personages from what is imagined by those who are not behind the scenes."

The appraisal process represents a small part of the scheme of things in the real estate world. In the private sector, all sorts of deals are made during the real estate acquisition or sale process. However, in government, accountability is required, and all deals must be scrutinized to ensure they are fair and proper. In recent years, the level of greed and corruption has been at an all-time high and has further been fueled by the significant increase in property values since the 1970s. I do not wish to disparage the many hardworking, competent people in government and its agencies. Many conscientious government and private sector employees are forced to work in programs that are not based on sound policies or in the best interest of the public.

The 1970s was a different era in Ontario for the overall working conditions, as employment standards and environmental regulations were lacking. Today, the working environment has largely changed, mainly due to complaints brought forward before the Human Rights Commission, and workplace regulations, that were introduced in 2000 – namely the Employment Standards Act.

Corporations, and the people employed by the corporations, that willfully cause damage or the death of human beings, should face the full consequences, and must rethink their agenda.

Most people have to work in order to provide for their families. They may be unaware of their employer's business practices, or chose to ignore them. A number of industries have polluted areas of the world, resulting in the deaths of people. Some corporations in North America, feeling that the laws are stacked against them, have decided to conduct their business overseas. A prime example is the Chevron incident which resulted in the contamination of Ecuador's Amazon rainforest by the dumping of 80,000 tons of oil and toxic residues, thereby ruining rivers and drinking water in a 19,305-square-mile area, and contributing to high cancer rates and birth defects among the local population. But there are many other examples worldwide.

The three most disastrous nuclear meltdowns were Three Mile Island (TMI), in Pennsylvania, Chernobyl, in Ukraine, and Fukushima, in Japan. The Three Mile Island accident was a partial nuclear meltdown that occurred on March 28, 1979, in reactor number 2 of the Three Mile Island nuclear generating station (TMI-2), in Dauphin County, Pennsylvania, United States. It was the worst accident in U.S. commercial nuclear power plant history, and was rated a five on the seven-point International Nuclear Event Scale. A cleanup started in August 1979, and officially ended in December 1993, with a total cleanup cost of about $1 billion. (Source: Wikipedia)

It is well known that lobbyists are used by corporations to continually lobby governments to facilitate their agenda, and to undertake business or controversial projects that are sometimes detrimental to the public. The lobbyists, and their clients, are able to open doors to politicians, which does not typically exist as an option for the average citizen.

But much more alarming are Economic Hit Men (EHM). EHM are highly paid professionals hired by the U.S. government, or its agencies, to cheat countries around the world out of trillions of dollars. Money is loaned from the World Bank, the U.S.

Agency for International Development, and other similar organizations for various developments in foreign countries, according to John Perkins, author of the book *Confessions of an Economic Hit Man*. The loans benefit mainly U.S. corporations who use natural resources and have control of the same to complete the developments. This leaves some countries with very significant debts, which they are incapable of paying back. As per Mr. Perkins, these corporations have tools which include fraudulent financial reports, rigged elections, extortion, payoffs, sex, and murder. If the ECMs are not successful, CIA-sanctioned jackals step in to finish the job, which could eventually result in assassinations. If that does not work, the U.S. military is used as a final resort.

According to Catherine Austin Fitts, president of Solari, Inc., and former Assistant Secretary of Housing during the George H. W. Bush presidency, "As the pieces fit together, we shared a horrifying epiphany: the banks, corporations and investors acting in each global region were the exact same players. They were a relatively small group that reappeared again and again in Russia, Eastern Europe, and Asia, accompanied by the same well-known accounting firms and law firms. Clearly, there was a global financial *coup d'etat* underway."

Some high-net worth individuals or businesses chose to shelter their wealth, as evidenced by various media reports, including a recent incident known as the "Panama Papers." The documents come from an influential Panama-based law firm which are reported to include 11.5 million internal records disclosing the financial secrets of heads of state, billionaires, drug lords, celebrities and others. Several countries have announced inquiries into the secretive world of offshore tax evasion.

In 2015, Rothschild & Co. paid a fine of $11.5 million to the U.S. Department of Justice, and avoided prosecution for helping Americans dodge taxes by using undeclared offshore accounts. Rothschild & Co. is among more than 80 Swiss banks that have paid about $80 billion to the U.S. government in penalties, fines, interest, and restitution. Recently, however, Rothschild is moving money in the reverse direction, by helping wealthy foreigners shelter their wealth in the U.S. through a trust company in Reno, Nevada. (Source: *Bloomberg Business Week* February 1-7, 2016)

Although Canada is regarded as one of the best countries in the world, one has to be able to retain the best lawyer, accountant, and investment advisor, to be informed about important business and tax matters. For some plaintiffs, the legal system can prove to be daunting or an uphill battle, and costly, unless there is a "smoking gun," or evidence *without a reasonable doubt.* Generally, the burden of proof rests with a plaintiff. I should know, as a plaintiff, the legal system in Ontario has caused me extreme grief due to financial losses, as outlined in this book.

In their efforts to get to the truth, journalists who seek answers are increasingly being hampered by political, legal, and bureaucratic barriers. Additional barriers are the costs and lengthy time period it takes to obtain the required information. In some instances, when the information is released, it is redacted.

Many people have already turned to alternative radio talk shows and Internet blogs to receive factual news that is lacking, or is under-reported in the mainstream media. There are numerous activists and watchdogs that exist today, which have had an impact on some of the food that is produced, items that are manufactured, and environmental matters. But some people seem to be uninformed, preoccupied with their own affairs, and relying on their leaders to do their job, or are so overwhelmed with all the negative news, that they have ignored important issues of the globalist elite, which has had an impact, and continues to impact, on the life of the majority.

When economic and other conditions warrant a new government, Canadians and Americans elect another political party, and toss out the old one. They hope the next party will deliver better results for the country than the previous one. How can this happen if the two main political parties in the U.S., and the main political parties in Canada, have close establishment ties? Many corporations, some with the assistance of their lobbyists, contribute to the political parties and lobby politicians to promote their agenda, which is usually not in the public interest. In addition, the level of corruption across the world is at an all-time high.

In the New World Order, workers are similar to a commodity. The unceasing improvement of machinery, which is developing ever more rapidly, makes the livelihood of workers more precarious. Their livelihood depends upon the success of firms or countries in global competition. The truth is that the big business market is corrupt. It's manipulated largely by self-interested *control-freaks*, and *too-big-to-go-to-jail* sociopaths, who want all the chips for themselves, and give only enough to you to keep you serving their interests and comforts. The logic of global capitalism is destroying the planet as it puts profits over the welfare of people, and excessive production over ecological sustainability. There have been massive protests against powerful institutions such as the World Bank, the International Monetary Fund, and the World Trade Organization, as well as so-called free trade deals which draw in more and more people who believe that a different model, which is sensitive to humans' needs and the environment, is required.

The tumultuous and divisive referendum campaign, on the future of the United Kingdom's place in the European Union, came to an end June 23, 2016, when voters decided to exit the European Union. The campaign process was interrupted by the tragic and violent murder of Labour MP Jo Cox who favoured the UK to remain in the EU. The results of the vote show an electorate divided by region, social class, and party affiliation. Generally, older people backed Brexit, while many of the younger generation, and affluent people, favoured staying in the EU, with London being a bastion of the Remain camp.

It is my opinion, if the world's population is not over-whelmingly united, the globalist agenda will flourish, and much of the population will experience what has been portrayed in movies such as *Soylent Green* and *Invasion of The Body Snatchers*, namely a marginalization of many people by government and corporations, and eventual elimination of some by a well-devised plan. A segment of the population in North America has already experienced marginalization due to losses of their savings, or because they have insufficient pensions. This does not take into consideration those who are already marginalized due to poverty, extreme handicap, or mental illness.

To know how human beings historically have treated one another, just look at the statistics of the two world wars. The total number of military and civilian casualties in World War I was more than 38 million. (Source: Wikipedia) World War II was the deadliest military conflict in history, in absolute terms of total dead. Over 60 million people were killed, but estimates of the total dead range from 50 million to more than 80 million. The higher figure includes deaths from war-related disease and famine. The total military dead were from 21 to 25 million. (Source: Wikipedia) Since the two world wars, the United States has been responsible for the deaths of reportedly between 20 and 30 million people in wars and conflicts scattered over the world (Source: Global Research) – and the pain and anger is spread even further. Some authorities estimate that there are as many as 10 wounded for each person who dies in wars. Their visible, continued suffering is a continuing reminder to their fellow countrymen. It is essential that Americans (and I would add, other war-mongering countries) learn more about this topic so that they can begin to understand the pain that others feel. (Source: Countercurrents.org)

CHAPTER 1

My First Office Job at The Ministry of Government Services

After I finished high school, I immigrated to Toronto in April 1973. It was a good time of the year to be in Toronto which facilitated my search for a job. I decided that employment in the provincial government would be a good start. I remember filing my application at the Frost Building, one of a complex of provincial government buildings at Queen's Park in downtown Toronto.

In August 1973, I was hired in a permanent position in the filing section of the Realty Services Department of the Ministry of Government Services, with its offices on the 13th floor of Ferguson Block, at Queen's Park, in Toronto. It was my first job – working in a full-time position in an office in Canada.

The provincial government was responsible for providing a variety of government services, and, in the 1970s, many ministries of the Ontario government had projects underway. Realty Services was one of those departments that required a variety of staff, such as surveyors, appraisers, negotiators, and clerical staff. It was somewhat of a different era in Ontario. Generally, it truly was a good time to be working in the government, and there seemed to be a lot of joyous days there. Some employees had issues, but the system functioned in spite of a few troublesome employees. The photograph below illustrates the management staff at MGS; the Director of Realty Services is absent.

The Managers and Chiefs of Appraising and Negotiations, photographed with Herb Spence, Assistant Director of Land Transfer. Back row (l-r): Maynard Millman, George Lee, Howard Leach, Roy Booth, Herb Spence. Front row (l-r): Bob Wolvin, Bob Wilson, Dom O'Connor

The senior management staff, that I remember working at MGS, included the following: Bill Gray, Director; Herb Spence, Assistant Director; Bob Wolvin, Manager of Sales & Acquisition; Dominic O'Connor, Manager; Bob Wilson, Manager of Sales; and George MacDonald, Manager of Appraisals.

My initial job as a clerk at MGS was interesting, as my supervisor, Jim McCullough, had a unique sense of humour which made working there pleasant. Also, I was constantly meeting many staff members who wanted to view department files for various realty projects in Ontario. As the weeks passed by, my curiosity of real estate began to grow sufficiently enough that I wanted to work as a real estate appraiser. The only way I could realize my desired ambition as a real estate appraiser was to start taking the required courses of the Appraisal Institute of Canada (AIC). I enrolled with the AIC in 1974 and commenced taking the courses. I requested a transfer to the appraisal section of the Ministry of Government Services, Realty Services Branch, and was given the opportunity to work there due to the recognition of my initiative by an assistant director, Herb Spence, and certain other staff who were very helpful in my promotion to the position of a real estate appraiser.

In about three years, I completed all of the required courses while I was working, and finished writing all of the examinations necessary by the Appraisal Institute of Canada at various locations, including one at Trent University, in Peterborough. But the toughest part of the AACI program was still ahead, including the need for five years of experience in appraisal work. The toughest part of the Appraisal Institute of Canada's real estate appraisal program was completing three demonstration appraisal reports of 75 to 100 pages, which was the equivalent of working on a thesis for three types of properties – one residential, and two investment properties – typically an apartment building and an industrial property. In April 1980, after five years of appraisal experience, the Appraisal Institute awarded me the Accredited Appraiser Canadian Institute (AACI) designation. I was told that I was one of the youngest people to complete the AACI program at that time.

The extent of my travel in Ontario was the widest possible, since I worked on appraisal assignments, or projects, in northern, southwestern, and Eastern Ontario. The types of projects included: the valuation of agricultural lands in the Bruce Peninsula for the provincial government's Niagara Escarpment; a variety of property types for the Parkway Belt West; the Ministry of the Environment's requirements, namely the valuation of easements and lands for lagoons; and the appraisal of district offices of the Ministry of Natural Resources and Ontario Provincial Police.

The first project that I worked on was in the Bruce Peninsula; it involved the appraisal of lands for the Niagara Escarpment. The Niagara Escarpment is a protected area under the Province of Ontario's Niagara Escarpment Planning and Development Act, 1973, and the Niagara Escarpment Plan (NEP), Canada's first large-scale environmental land use plan. The Niagara Escarpment Plan outlines land use designations, development criteria, and related permitted uses, including farming, forestry, and mineral resource extraction.

Working on the Niagara Escarpment project was one of my most enjoyable projects, since a number of government appraisers and negotiators worked during the weekdays, as a team, out of the Holiday Inn Hotel, in Owen Sound. Typically, I would drive on Mondays from Toronto to Owen Sound, and be assigned files by my supervisor which required obtaining comparable sales to estimate the value of the individual subject properties, and to prepare appraisal reports. A great deal of patience was required for the registry office search portion of the assignment, as I would have to spend a significant amount of time in the registry office in Walkerton, Ontario. They were not automated as they are today. That meant having to request and wait for individual deeds, or transfer documents, and other documents while they were being extracted from the filing cabinets by the registry office staff. One could request up to only ten documents at a time, which was a slow process. In addition, after obtaining a deed, I had to obtain a reference plan, provided a survey had been done by the property owner; otherwise, I had to prepare a sketch based on a metes and bound description in the document. Sometimes, the description was very lengthy. My geographic area in the Bruce Peninsula included the Townships of Lindsay and Eastnor. I remember the enjoyable times had by all of my team in Owen Sound when we would get together after work and relate our experiences of the day, or previous weeks, or commiserate about other issues in our lives. Sometimes I would drive a few colleagues back to their hotel, as they had had a few too many drinks. Having the Ontario Provincial Police station near the hotel may have helped keep certain individuals sober enough during the week. I survived the Bruce Peninsula project and soon found myself working in other areas of Ontario, often independently.

Below is a picturesque view of the Holiday Inn, in the Town of Kenora, where I stayed during my travel to northwestern Ontario in the 1970s. The hotel is operating now as Clarion Inn Lakeside & Conference Centre.

An assignment I vividly remember is when I had to drive back from Kenora to Thunder Bay, in winter. Fortunately, a colleague, Peter Libiak, who worked out of the provincial government's Thunder Bay office, was in Kenora at the time. He suggested it would be prudent to drive back to Thunder Bay in his car, and I quickly took him up on his offer due to a heavy snowstorm in the area. The snowstorm had abated and we were fortunate enough to reach a small community known as Upsala, which is about one and a half hour's drive from Thunder Bay. However, the severe snowstorm had impacted the entire region and made most roads impassable. As we did not want to risk our lives driving at night on a snow-bound highway, we decided it would be wise to stay in a motel. However, we quickly found out that no accommodation was available in Upsala. The local motel owner informed us that a local church had volunteered to let stranded motorists stay overnight in Upsala United Church. We were able to obtain a couple of sleeping bags and spent the night in a church. During the middle of the night, we heard a knock on the church door. When my friend answered it, a young couple said that they had heard we were letting stranded people stay in the church, to which my friend replied that we were one of those stranded people, and they were welcome to stay there. The couple came into the church and disappeared behind a curtain at the altar. Below is an exterior view of the church where my colleague and I had to stay overnight due to the area snowstorm. The handwriting on the photo is that of Peter Libiak.

My Own True Story

My travels to northern Ontario brought me closer to nature. But I experienced something else I had never known before. The life of some of the aboriginal, or indigenous, Canadians really shocked me, as I saw them battle one or more of the following: alcoholism, malnutrition, or disease. The Canadian Human Rights Tribunal's ruling, in January 2016, denunciated Canada for its long-standing racial discrimination against Indigenous children. The multiple suicides in Attawapiskat in 2016 represent a growing list of over 600 young people who have considered, or attempted, suicide since 2009 in the northern part of the Ontario riding of Charlie Angus, the NDP Indigenous Affairs critic, and Member of Parliament from Timmins-James Bay. It seems there is nothing accidental about a culture of discrimination that has been entrenched since Confederation. On many occasions, Health Canada and Indian Affairs reportedly turned down pleas for mental health services and suicide counselling. (Source: OurWindsor.Ca, February 19, 2016)

Another assignment I was asked to go on was to establish the rent of Crown land for Bell Canada's microwave towers, in remote areas, north of Red Lake. That involved flying from Toronto to Ear Falls. From Red Lake, I was able to secure the services of the local Ministry of Natural Resources, to travel by amphibious, or float plane, onward to North Spirit Lake and Big Trout Lake, where the Bell Canada microwave tower sites were to be located. Fortunately, I had an experienced pilot and the flight went well. The Ministry of Natural Resources was very helpful in the completion of many of my assignments.

The coldest location during my winter assignments was Kapuskasing. I remember staying at Northern Lights Motel. When I attempted to start my car the next morning, I mistakenly removed my winter glove and touched the ignition switch, which resulted in my fingers being stuck to the switch due to the extreme cold temperature of minus 30 degrees Celsius. I

7

panicked, but soon realized the battery of my car was dead. I quickly found out how my car could function again with a battery boost from the local auto repair garage. They also informed me it was prudent to install a block heater in my car.

An interesting appraisal assignment was the Burwash Industrial Farm, on Highway 69, about 40 km south of the City of Sudbury. It comprised a former prison farm that was established in 1914, based on the revolutionary premise that low-risk inmates would benefit from the exercise and skills learned while working outdoors at self-supporting institutions. At the time it was established, Burwash Industrial Farm reflected up-to-date penal philosophy, which recognized the former practice of building fortified prisons for all classes of inmates as being both expensive and unscientific. The farm occupied 35,000 acres of owned land and 101,000 acres of leased land, where 600 to 1,000 people, including prison staff and their families, lived. Burwash Industrial Farm accommodated between 180 and 820 minimum and medium security offenders. It was closed in 1975 due to changes in correctional practices. About 30% of the total area was leased for various uses. A small portion of the farm, known as Camp Bison, was sold to the federal government.

A planning/consulting firm had identified the most appropriate use of Burwash Farm as an integrated maximum and minimum security prison, with cattle enterprise and selected recreational uses designed to permit wildlife management. (Source: Burwash, Ontario Heritage Trust)

This assignment was complicated, as the key issue was trying to determine the highest and best use of a large holding in a sparsely populated area of Ontario. But the other aspect was determining internal government needs – financial, ecological and political. The buildings were demolished when the site became a Department of National Defence training ground in the mid-1980s. Incidentally, other industrial farms in Ontario were in Fort William (Thunder Bay area), which opened in 1911, Langstaff (Yonge Street and Highway 7 area), Concord (in Vaughan), in 1912, and Mimico (Etobicoke), in 1913.

Looking back, I believe the toughest assignments were: the valuation of D'Arcy Place in the Town of Cobourg, a former armed forces depot consisting of residential and recreational buildings; Hamilton Courthouse; Arrell Observation & Detention Home in Hamilton; Kawartha Lakes Training School, a youth reformatory in Lindsay; the valuation of 85,510 acres of land on Cockburn Island for an exchange with a paper manufacturing company; and the preparation of a feasibility study of land, with road access versus lake access for proposed cottage lots on Obonga Lake, near Armstrong, north of Thunder Bay. Below is a photograph of me standing next to the helicopter that took me from Thunder Bay to Armstrong, to enable me to view the land holding at Obonga Lake.

ME IN MY 20'S NEXT TO THE HELICOPTER USED TO FLY FROM THUNDER BAY TO ARMSTRONG

Mel H. Castelin

I would consider one of the most memorable recreational areas I worked in as being Wasaga Beach, where I had to prepare appraisals of properties for Wasaga Beach Provincial Park. The Town of Wasaga Beach is located in the County of Simcoe, along the southern end of Georgian Bay.

Georgian Bay provides Wasaga Beach with the longest freshwater beach in the world, namely 14 kilometres of sandy beach on Nottawasaga Bay. During the late 1970s, the market value of many cottage lots was $5,000, and cottages could be purchased for about $10,000. Today's property values have increased very significantly, and there is a presence of biker gangs and drug dealers in town. I was approached by a typical biker who revved his motor bike to get my attention; it was obvious to him from my license plate (which advertised the car dealership) that I was from out-of-town. During the 1940's, undesirables and juvenile gangs came to the beach area for parties. By the 1950's, they were replaced by motorcycle gangs who would use the hard packed sand for races. To cater to the transient population, many commercial establishments began to open up along the beach. Many cottages were built for, or by, those who became the seasonal residents of Wasaga Beach. The incorporation of the Town of Wasaga Beach was effective on January 1, 1974, with expanded borders. The local population was relatively small in comparison with the number of people that visited Wasaga Beach in the summer, which was estimated at over two million. (Source: Town of Wasaga Beach Profile)

Other special use property appraisals, or reports, that I prepared were for the following:

• Allandale Golf Course, a 9 hole, 36 par course in Painswick (Township of Innisfil)

- A summer retreat of 1,340 acres in Misery Bay, Manitoulin Island, which I had to appraise one winter with access by snowmobile
- St. Joseph's School, and St. Mary's School, in Barrie
- An economic analysis and valuation of the surplus lands of ten properties in the City of London, including the London Psychiatric Hospital, Ministry of Transportation's patrol yards, and Byron Children's Psychiatric Research Institute
- A realty sales survey and economic analysis of the surplus lands of twelve properties in the City of Thunder Bay, including the Lakehead Psychiatric Hospital, court house, adult training centre, district jail, and the Ministry of Natural Resources' Current River Air Base

In the 1970's, I actually enjoyed being on the road and seeing various communities in Ontario. Every week had something new to offer, and it was an exciting life. Some of the assignments involved driving as far as North Bay, or flying to Sudbury or Thunder Bay. But events began to change in the civil service by the early 1980's. I had reached a point where the working environment in that government department changed for the worse; some employees had resigned and joined other employers. In addition, there was a lot of office politics and I was being given assignments in Northern Ontario, inordinately more often than other staff, most likely because I was not married and did not complain about the assignments handed to me. The majority of the employees were a lot older than me. In addition, a number of staff consumed a heck of a lot of booze, and I did not fit in that environment. Some would have "liquid lunches" at noon, and even go back to work afterword. Eventually, the work environment for me became an unpleasant one. In addition, there were a lot of complaints by staff to their supervisors or management, "back-stabbing" and vendettas harboured by certain staff.

Mel H. Castelin

The staff and management would not have been able to make derogatory comments or verbalize their thoughts in the manner expressed during office hours in the 1970s, without being reprimanded or being faced with consequences. I was 20 years old when I started to work in the provincial government. It definitely was a different era in Ontario with respect to a number of issues, including the overall working atmosphere, a lack of employment standards and environmental regulations, and perpetual conflict between management and some staff.

Today, the working environment has changed to an extent in the provincial government due to workplace regulations that were introduced in 2000, namely the Employment Standards Act, and because of the Human Rights Commission. The incident that comes to my mind is, even though appraisers were required to work in the field in inclement weather, namely minus 20 or 30 degrees Celsius, proper boots and winter coats were not supplied by the government. It was only after an employee found out that there was a provision in the Ministry's policy manual to reimburse staff for these essential items, that we were reimbursed for a winter coat. I remember wearing an inadequate winter coat and shoes during my many trips to Northern Ontario during winter in the 1970s; it is a miracle I survived working during winter in Northern Ontario.

A colleague, with whom I had worked on several assignments during the 1970s, obtained permission to work after he turned 65 years of age. We had got along well and worked together on several projects in the Ministry of Government Services. Unfortunately, he had a rough time working there, as he had a hearing impediment in one ear, and appeared confrontational at times due to his war-related experiences. He told me he was unable to accomplish his desire to become a lawyer. He finally succumbed to a debilitating illness at a nursing home, a terrible condition to be in.

The Evolution of the Ministry of Government Services

By the early 1990s, the Ministry of Government Services ceased to be the ministry that managed the real estate requirements of the provincial government. The Ontario Realty Corporation (ORC) was established in 1993 as a Crown corporation under the Capital Investment Plan Act, 1993. ORC provided real estate, property, and project management services to most ministries and agencies of the province of Ontario. It was based in Toronto.

Since June 2005, ORC had reported to the Minister of Public Infrastructure Renewal. Management of real property and accommodations was a responsibility shared by the Ministry of Public Infrastructure Renewal (PIR), ORC, and its client ministries and agencies. As a service provider, ORC itself owned no real estate. The majority of the assets it managed were for the owner, represented by the Ministry of PIR, which provided it with direction, funding, and approvals for significant decisions regarding those assets. ORC managed one of Canada's largest real estate portfolios. Eighty-one percent of the portfolio was owned by the government of Ontario, and the remainder was leased. Statistics indicate in the 2005/06 fiscal year, it employed approximately 300 staff.

When the Conservatives won the provincial election in Ontario in 1995, the government changed the focus of the province's real estate department, from improving and developing public lands, to selling them. This major shift in policy was designed to generate quick revenue so the government could balance its budget and implement tax cuts. It led to the sale of hundreds of millions of dollars of real estate assets by ORC. However, by 1999, ORC President, Tony Miele, began raising concerns about irregularities in land deals and environmental clean-up costs prior to the sales. This led to a major internal audit which showed widespread problems with numerous ORC transactions. The opposition Liberal and NDP parties claimed the Conservative government was selling the province's lands cheap, in *sweetheart deals.*

As of June 6, 2011, Ontario Realty Corporation was acquired by Ontario Infrastructure and Lands Corporation. It offered construction project management, facilities management, strategic portfolio management, and asset rationalization services on behalf of the Government of Ontario and its client ministries. The company also provided strategic asset management, project services, and heritage management process and class environmental assessment services, as well as portfolio management services, including property services. In addition, it offered professional services, such as environment and cultural heritage, land use planning, accessibility planning, appraisals, surveys, green buildings/sustainability, and property inventory information services.

Criminal Probe Targeted Staff at Ontario Realty Corporation

The Ministry of the Attorney General and ORC had sued reportedly more than 50 individuals and companies for $48 million, in the year 2000, for damages for their alleged role in fraud, conspiracy, bid rigging, negligence, forgery, kickbacks, and breach of contract, in about 40 land sales and contracts at ORC in the 1990s. The number of defendants was eventually pared down to a few, in an odyssey that took over eight years to make it to court. One of the defendants had obtained a parcel of industrial land of about 27 acres in Brampton, in a sale by ORC in 1999, for $90,000 while appraisers had valued it for more than $1.6 million. The same defendant reportedly obtained a parcel of about 29 acres in Mississauga in a bidding process for $2.2 million, even though another company reportedly submitted a higher bid. That defendant then sought a reduction in the price of the land for environmental clean-up, and sold the land 14 months later for $4.3 million, resulting in a profit to the defendant of $2.4 million. The same defendant also bought a site of about 88 acres in Bowmanville for $1.7 million, but gained a reduction of $600,000 for the cost of sewer and storm connections, although terms of the agreement disallowed it. Two former ORC employees pleaded guilty to criminal charges of accepting kickbacks. One employee had to pay back $100,000 for conferring a benefit to a public official, while another employee paid back $85,000 in kickbacks which he had reportedly buried in a relatives backyard.

In 2004, the Ontario Provincial Police Anti-Rackets Section charged three men with fraud-related offences pertaining to environmental cleanup contracts.

According to a report from Canada News Wire, environmental contracts and environmental cleanup work were being improperly tendered, fraudulent real estate sales were being conducted, and kickbacks were being made to government employees associated with former employees of the Ontario Realty Corporation. A self-employed environmental engineer based in Brooklin, Ontario, was charged with seven counts of fraud, twelve counts of forgery, and five counts of fraud on the government associated to the payment of rewards. Two other ORC employees were also charged – one of them with one count of breach of trust, seven counts of act upon forged document, four counts of fraud on the government for accepting a reward, and one count of fraud; the second employee in Toronto was charged with one count of breach of trust, three counts of fraud on the government for accepting a reward, and six counts of act upon forged documents. The accused were all released on a *Promise to Appear* at Old City Hall, on October 18, 2004.

ORC had named a new president and CEO, namely David Glass, several months after the resignation of the previous chief, Tony Miele, who resigned in February 2006. Mr. Miele reorganized and downsized ORC after it was plagued by allegations of widespread bid-rigging, conspiracy, fraud, and bribery, in a series of land sales and environmental contracts. Mr. Miele was credited with revamping ORC following suspicious land deals that sparked an OPP probe, resulting in a forensic audit of about 2,800 land transactions dating back to 1985. That probe resulted in one former ORC employee being convicted of accepting kickbacks and breach of trust, and others facing charges. Staff at the Ontario government's real-estate arm, Ontario Realty Corporation, were under criminal investigation as part of a probe involving public-sector employees' financial dealings with private-sector firms. The probe also involved employees in government ministries, though it was unclear which ones.

Government sources stressed that the probe was confined to employees in the public sector, and that no MPPs or political staff were swept up in it. The OPP had confirmed that the OPP's anti-rackets division was investigating allegations of "irregular" transactions between government employees and suppliers of goods and services. OPP officers, equipped with search warrants, had raided government offices in the Macdonald Block, near the provincial legislature. The ORC's offices were in the complex. One area of the OPP's focus was one of the ministry's *capital and accommodation services branch*, which was responsible for strategic planning, project management, and dealing with the Ministry of Energy and Infrastructure.

Even though no political staff were involved in the investigation, it was difficult for the McGuinty government to distance itself from a developing situation that became its biggest scandal since eHealth. The spending scandal at eHealth

Ontario involved an arm's length government agency. At eHealth Ontario there was lavish spending on consultants by an arm's length government agency. The scandal dogged the provincial government during much of the summer of 2009, and ultimately led to the resignation of former health minister David Caplan, and a probe by the provincial auditor, who highlighted the role that Premier Dalton McGuinty played at eHealth. The findings of Ontario Auditor General Jim McCarter into eHealth Ontario that were released in late 2009 indicated a spending scandal whereby successive governments wasted $1 billion in taxpayer money. (Source: CBC News, October 7, 2009)

Ontario Realty Corp. managed one of the largest real estate portfolios in Canada on behalf of the provincial government. Assets owned or leased by the Crown agency consisted of vacant land as well as more than 6,000 buildings, including office towers, heritage buildings, courthouses and jails. The ORC had a large bureaucracy of a reported 117 executives who reportedly made between $100,000 and $482,000.

By 2008, ORC had hired three project management firms, MHPM, CB Richard Ellis, and SNC-Lavalin ProFac, to deliver services in different parts of Ontario, according to ORC's spokesman, Bill Moore. They were to be a buffer between ORC staff and private contractors. Toronto-based CB Richard Ellis Canada, a major commercial real estate company, was selected by ORC to handle all its responsibilities in 2009. At that time, it inherited several hundred employees working on government contracts. The vice-chairman of CB Richard Ellis was John O'Bryan at that time. The outsourcing move led to a downsizing of staff in the ORC central office in Toronto, and the removal of staff. Contractors, who regularly dealt with the government, had complained to provincial officials during 2009/2010 about competitors gaining unusual favourable attention in winning work.

Mel H. Castelin

Ministry of Transportation and Ontario Realty Corporation Raided in OPP Probe

Staff at the Ontario Ministry of Transportation were under criminal investigation as part of a probe into "irregular" financial dealings with the private sector, and the ministry had been identified as one of several raided by the Ontario Provincial Police. The OPP had said the investigation involved "irregular transactions" between government staff and outside contractors. OPP spokespersons said the force had not arrested or charged anyone, as of yet, in the probe. A source familiar with the probe said that OPP officers, armed with search warrants, arrived at the Transportation Ministry's offices, where they examined computer files dealing with the purchase of goods and services from private-sector suppliers. The raid also involved Ontario Realty Corporation, and a government official confirmed that employees at the Ontario government's real estate arm were also under investigation. OPP officials said the force's anti-rackets branch, which handled complex fraud investigations, had launched a probe into "irregular financial transactions" involving unnamed government ministries and outside suppliers. At that time, many questions remained unanswered about the probe, including just how many public sector employees were under investigation. It was not known which other ministries were involved.

It was not the first time ORC employees were embroiled in controversy. The Ontario government spent about $23 million in legal and consultant fees pursuing a long-running case dating back to 2000, and involving allegations of bid rigging and fraud at ORC. The government sued four ORC employees and a group of outside contractors in 2000 for more than $35 million relating to about 40 transactions. After pursuing the case for more than seven years, lawyers acting for the government ended up going after seven of the transactions. Two ORC employees and one contractor pleaded guilty to a variety of criminal offences, including accepting kickbacks and forging bids. All three agreed to make restitution and received conditional sentences with no jail time.

Summary

Working in the 1970s, in the Ministry of Government Services, was an exciting and challenging task for me. My valuation experience was the widest I have experienced, and I had the opportunity of travelling all over Ontario. Eventually, some older staff retired, while others fell ill or succumbed to an early demise. The work environment began to change in the 1980s, which was precipitated by changing technology, an aging workforce in the branch, and the government having accomplished a great deal of its objectives with respect to land acquisition for highways, parks, the environment, and various other purposes. In addition, there were cutbacks, and the impact of think-tanks, or consultants, who felt the government and the taxpayer would be better served by contracting much of the work done by civil servants to the private sector, such as private sector planning firms and fee appraisal companies. But, as evidenced by details herein, the level of fraud and corruption was at its greatest level in the 1990s and 2000s, after significant staff cutbacks and contracting out of services. The Ontario government had reportedly paid about $23.4 million for outside lawyers (over 52% of the total fees), forensic accountants and consulting firms in pursuit of corruption allegations in one civil case from March 2000 to December 2008.

In hindsight, starting work at a young age was beneficial. However, as I spent long hours working and travelling to remote or distant locations in Ontario, I began to feel de-humanized in a work environment that was poisoned. Although I received on-the-job training and exposure to a wide variety of appraisal assignments, much of my work was self-taught from being exposed to field work or travelling to various communities in the province of Ontario. I was really lucky, as many staff died early in their retirement, and some before their retirement, from health complications due to alcoholism and other illnesses. But I paid a heavy price during the last year of my tenure at the Ministry of Government Services due to a toxic work environment that was created by improper management practices, and all sorts of office politics, combined with a lack of proper nutrition, while I was on the road from 1974 to 1980. Subsequently, I opted to leave the Ministry of Government Services due to my overwhelming frustration with certain staff and the difficulties faced by me in gaining promotions and acceptance in the workplace. I felt a change in employers was essential for my well-being, and decided to apply for employment elsewhere in the provincial government.

The next chapter provides some details of the next cycle in my career which commenced in 1981.

Sources: October 27, 2004 by Hazmat Management; Detective Superintendent Rick Kotwa; Karen Howlett and Adam Radwanski, *The Globe and Mail,* July 17, 2010 and July 19, 2010; *Toronto Star,* August 26, 2006, October 23, 2008, February 9, 2009; Tony Van Alphen, Kevin Donovan, Robert Benzie, *Toronto Star* staff reporters, published July 19, 2010; with files from Isabel Teotonio, Tanya Talaga and Tony Wong

CHAPTER 2

The Next Cycle of My Employment Career

In 1981, I was successful in applying for a real estate appraisal position with the Ministry of Housing where I was employed from 1981 to 1983. The office was a much smaller one than my previous employer's, and the department comprised less than a dozen staff. The office manager was Stan Purves who I found to be pleasant to work for and a decent person; we got along well.

I found myself working more independently. The work was quite complex and somewhat different to what I had been working on in the previous years, as it primarily involved estimating the total costs for social housing projects, namely senior citizen and family housing projects in Ontario. Some of my work involved rental conversion projects and the analysis of rents and operating costs of various multi-unit buildings in various areas of Ontario.

Social housing refers to rental housing developed with the assistance of the government, and subsidized by the government for people with low to moderate incomes, seniors, or people with special needs who can live, with supports, in the community.

In 1938, the National Housing Act was passed into Federal law. In 1946, the Social Safety Net legislation was enacted. In 1948, Ontario passed the Ontario Housing Development Act. In the 1950s, the Local Housing Authorities were established, starting out as single-family dwellings. In 1964, the National Housing Act was revised, and the Ontario Housing Corporation (OHC) was founded to enable Ontario to manage its own public housing. The OHC was established under the Ontario Housing Corporation Act, funded by rental income and provincial and federal subsidies. During the 1970s, in Ontario, a great deal of money was invested into constructing large apartment buildings and duplexes. The 1980s were marked by the federal government promoting non-profit and co-op housing through the Canada Mortgage and Housing Corporation. In 1998, Consolidated Municipal Service Managers took on the financial costs of social housing. The year 2000 was marked by the dissolution of the Ontario Housing Corporation and the introduction of the Social Housing Reform Act of Ontario. Source: Wikipedia

Built in the early 1950s, the first social housing project in Canada was Regent Park, in Toronto, and was funded by the City of Toronto with provincial and federal contributions. Regent Park, Canada's largest publicly funded housing development, and home to about 7,500 people, has recently undergone a massive revitalization program.

Ontario's housing programs are summarized below. Sources: CMHC; Ministry of Housing

1964-1979 – Public Housing Program

- Subsidized housing owned by the Province of Ontario through the Ontario Housing Corporation (OHC)
- Managed by 54 Local Housing Authorities (LHAs) across the province
- Cost-shared by the provincial and federal governments

- Public housing developments ranged from single family homes to large apartment complexes
- There were approximately 84,000 households living in public housing in Ontario
- The provincial government stopped building public housing in the late 1970's in favour of supporting the development of smaller, community-based non-profits and co-ops

1973-1978 – Non-Profit and Co-operative Housing Program

- Mixed income housing projects (both rent-geared-to-income and market units) were built through the sponsorship of community-based non-profit corporations
- Funded by the federal government through Central Mortgage and Housing Corporation (CMHC)
- The provincial government provided rent subsidy funding
- Over 135,000 households lived in housing which was owned and managed by local non-profit housing groups

1978-1985 – Co-operative & Private Non-Profit Housing Program

- A continuation of the mixed income housing program
- Housing sponsored by community-based, non-profit housing corporations
- Built using program funding from Canada Mortgage and Housing Corporation (CMHC), with rent subsidy assistance from the Province

1979-1985 – Municipal Non-Profit Housing Program

- Tri-partite agreements signed by the federal, provincial, and municipal governments

- Program designed to support an active municipal role in the provision of housing for people with low to moderate incomes

1986-1993 – Federal/Provincial Non-Profit Housing Program

- A federal/provincial cost-sharing program to provide housing for people with low and moderate incomes

The diagram below illustrates the assistance provided by various levels of government for social housing in Ontario from 1978 to 1995. Source: Ontario Non-Profit Housing Association – Timeline: A History of Social Housing in Ontario.

Most of my work with the Ministry of Housing involved estimating the total price of non-profit housing projects in Ontario, and ensuring a project was within the maximum unit price (MUP), as established by the Ministry of Housing. This involved either cross-checking a proponent's submission to ensure it was within the MUP, or developing a breakdown of the price of the major components of a building, and adding the land component to arrive at a total price of the project. A project was rarely allowed to proceed if the MUP was exceeded. If a housing project was in excess of the MUP, the Ministry's coordinator and the developer would dialogue to find where the costs excess existed, and would find ways to curtail some costs to ensure the project was within the MUP. The key issue was that developers were required to build modest housing, and not semi-luxury or luxury buildings, as the government was funding the project. Over the years, various incentives were introduced to attract developers to build social housing projects. The section of the ministry that I worked at was headed by a manager by the name of Stan Purves.

Some of the non-profit housing projects completed by me included the following:

- 187 unit senior citizen's housing complex in Toronto
- Regent Park Community Centre, Toronto
- 181 unit senior citizens' housing complex in North York
- senior citizens' housing complex in Stratford
- senior citizens' housing complex in Wiarton
- senior citizens' housing complex in Sioux Lookout
- senior citizens' housing complex in North Bay
- senior citizens' housing complex in Kenora

Eventually, I found I was being affected by the internal working environment. The work was complicated by a dysfunctional office, created by a lack of comradery between certain staff and a manager, who was very reasonable but whose function was not appreciated by a few troublesome employees. However, a more serious problem emanated, namely a lack of adequate funding for non-profit housing, which created a further burden for the department and some of the staff.

Working for the Ministry of Housing was a challenging task for me. However, the work environment began to change due to a lack of funding for housing projects, and because the government had accomplished a great deal of its initial objectives with respect to providing social housing. The decline in my work environment, combined with the long hours of work, travel in Ontario, and the completion of many cost estimates for social housing, had had an impact on my health, and contributed to my acute stress. Fortunately, I survived, and, in 1984, I eventually found myself back at the Ministry of Government Services where I was able to secure work as an appraiser/negotiator. But I could not see myself working there for more than about two years, and attempted to seek employment elsewhere, as evidenced by the details that follow.

My first vacation in May 1981 at the Yankee Clipper Hotel in Fort Lauderdale, Florida.

The history of Fort Lauderdale, Florida began more than 4,000 years ago with the arrival of the first aboriginal natives, and later with the Tequesta Indians, who inhabited the area for more than a thousand years. Though control of the area changed among Spain, England, the United States, and the Confederate States of America, it remained largely undeveloped until the 20th century. The first settlement in the area was the site of a massacre at the beginning of the Second Seminole War, an event which precipitated the abandonment of the settlement, and set back development in the area by over 50 years. The first United States stockade, named Fort Lauderdale, was built in 1838, and subsequently was a site of fighting during the Second Seminole War. The fort was abandoned in 1842, after the end of the war, and the area remained virtually unpopulated until the 1890s.

The Fort Lauderdale area was known as the *New River Settlement,* prior to the 20th century. While a few pioneer families had lived in the area since the late 1840s, it was not until the Florida East Coast Railroad built tracks through the area in the mid-1890s that any organized development began. The city was incorporated in 1911, and in 1915 was designated the county seat of newly formed Broward County.

Fort Lauderdale's first major development began in the 1920s, during the Florida land boom of the 1920s. The 1926 Miami hurricane, and the Great Depression of the 1930s, caused a great deal of economic dislocation. When World War II began, Fort Lauderdale became a major US Navy base, with a Naval Air Station to train pilots, radar and fire control operator training schools, and a Coast Guard base at Port Everglades. After the war ended, service members returned to the area, spurring an enormous population explosion which dwarfed the 1920s boom. In the 1970s, Fort Lauderdale beach became a mecca for runaways, and a group of approximately 60 to 150 runaways formed a group called *The Family.* Most resorted to petty crimes to support themselves and others.

In 1946, the Navy decommissioned its airfields in the area; Naval Air Station Fort Lauderdale became Broward County International Airport (later Fort Lauderdale-Hollywood International Airport), and West Prospect Field became Fort Lauderdale Executive Airport, the eleventh busiest general aviation airport in the country.

One year later, the 1947 Fort Lauderdale hurricane, an unusually large (120 mile radius) Category 4 hurricane, came ashore just north of the city, causing extensive damage due to flooding. Earlier storms that year had saturated the ground, and the tremendous rainfall from this slow-moving storm left the city (and much of the state) under several inches of water for weeks.

In the 1950s, the city became a favorite destination for college students for spring break, a tradition immortalized in the 1960 film *Where the Boys Are*. Every year in February, March, and April, tens of thousands of college students would come to relax at the beaches, and party at the many bars along A1A.

A 1967 report estimated that the city was approximately 85% developed, and the 1970 population figure was 139,590. After 1970, as Fort Lauderdale became essentially built out, growth in the area shifted to suburbs to the west. As cities such as Coral Springs, Miramar, and Pembroke Pines experienced explosive growth, Fort Lauderdale's population stagnated, and the city actually shrank by almost 4,000 people. A slight rebound brought the population back up to 152,397 at the 2000 census. Since 2000, Fort Lauderdale has gained slightly over 18,000 residents through annexation of seven neighborhoods in unincorporated Broward County.

Beginning in 1986, with the passage of a bond issue, the city of Fort Lauderdale began an aggressive effort to connect the city's arts and entertainment district, the historic downtown area, and the Las Olas shopping and beach district, to shake its long-standing reputation as a cultural wasteland and college-student party town.

The centerpiece of the cultural renaissance was the Riverwalk project, which runs along the New River from the Broward Center for the Performing Arts to the Stranahan House, with work in progress to extend the walk to Las Olas Boulevard. The Museum Of Art, which moved into its current location in

1986, and the Museum of Discovery and Science, which opened in its current location in 1992, are cornerstones of the Riverwalk project. A number of upscale high-rise residential towers along the river have encouraged the development of high-end shopping and entertainment throughout the downtown region.

After a rowdy 1985 spring break season, in which an estimated 350,000 college tourists caused disruption for several weeks in the spring, the city passed a series of restrictive laws in an effort to reduce the mayhem caused by the spring break throngs, and the mayor, Robert Dressler, appeared on *Good Morning America* to tell college students they were no longer welcome in Fort Lauderdale. Overnight parking was banned near the beach, and an open-container law prohibiting the consumption of alcohol in public places was enacted. The following spring, the city denied MTV a permit to set up their stage on the beach, and approximately 2,500 people were arrested as the new laws were strictly enforced. In 1985, 350,000 college students spent about $110 million during the nine-week spring break season; by 2004, 700,000 visitors, mostly families or European tourists, spent $800 million during the same period. By 2006, the number of college students visiting for spring break was estimated at approximately 10,000.

Source: Wikipedia - History of Fort Lauderdale

Fort Lauderdale is a pleasant location to spend one's vacation, and I liked the area so much in 1981 that I tried my best to move there. The only feasible way to accomplish this objective was to secure a job there. But I had no idea of the obstacles that awaited me.

I searched for job openings and was able to find a position with the Department of Transportation (DOT) in Fort Lauderdale. At that time, I had obtained the American equivalent of the AACI designation, namely the Senior Real Property Appraiser (SRPA) designation which was granted to me by the American Appraisal Institute. After several attempts to call and write to a number of individuals with the DOT, I was asked to attend an interview with Roy Fisher, Chief District Review Appraiser with the DOT. I arranged a flight to Fort Lauderdale for my interview, and met with Mr. Fisher who welcomed me to his office. After my successful interview, he took his staff and me for lunch at a local restaurant. Later in the afternoon, he showed me some sea manatee feeding at a local aquarium. As a result of a successful interview with the DOT, I was formerly awarded the position of a Review Appraiser (Right of Way Specialist III) in May 1984.

At the time of my job search, I had obtained and filled out the relevant initial application form to work in the United States. I took the completed form to the US Consulate on University Avenue in Toronto. The US Consulate instantly declined my application based on the fact that I had no parents or spouse residing in the US.

In order to legally work in the US, I had to obtain a Green Card. However, in order to speed up the process, I retained a US based immigration lawyer by the name of Bernard Rosenbloom, who was associated with Harry A. De Mell, an attorney at law in New York. He tried his best to secure the DOT position in Fort Lauderdale. However, the DOT was unable to keep the position open indefinitely, as they had a project to undertake, namely the Port Everglades Expressway which was to extend from Naples in the west, to Fort Lauderdale in the east, with one of the sections of the expressway known as the *Alligator Alley* project. The engineering firms responsible for construction of the project were Raymond Kaiser Engineers, a subsidiary of Raymond International Inc., and Howard Needles Tammen & Bergendoff (HNTB). HNTB Corporation is an architecture, civil engineering consulting and construction management firm that was founded in 1914. Its headquarters are in Kansas City, Missouri, but the firm has numerous offices across the United States. The firm has designed many bridges, roadways, airports, professional sports stadiums and rail and transit systems across the United States and around the world.

Much to my disappointment, I was unable to obtain a temporary visa, in spite of retaining an immigration lawyer and the DOT categorically stating that they were unable to find a US qualified appraiser for the job based on the numerous applications they had received at that time.

Having consumed so much time pursuing employment in the US, finding out that I could not work there was disappointing to me, especially since my search process had taken about three years. In August 1985, I made one final attempt at applying for a position in the US, namely with the City of New York. However, the City of New York informed me that an applicant had to be a resident of the United States and reside in New York City.

Summary

The DOT was dependent on state funding to accomplish its objectives for highway construction projects. Even though I was qualified to do the work at the DOT, obtaining a temporary visa to work in the US was a hurdle I was not able to accomplish. The DOT was not able to keep the position I had applied for open indefinitely, and ultimately hired someone who moved to Florida from another state.

The next chapter will provide details of what I proposed to do after encountering a number of obstacles in my employment career.

CHAPTER 3

My Position at Ontario Hydro as Senior Appraiser/Negotiator

For those not familiar with Ontario Hydro, it was one of the biggest publicly owned electric power utilities in the world. It was established in 1906 as the Hydro-Electric Power Commission of Ontario. Ontario Hydro was owned by the Government of Ontario, and effectively had a monopoly for generation and distribution of electricity in the Province of Ontario. Ontario Hydro operated twenty of the unique Canadian CANDU reactors, which have had both very good performance, and bad. Ontario Hydro used to get about two thirds of its power from nuclear. Ontario Hydro was formed to build transmission lines to supply municipal utilities with electricity generated by private companies already operating at Niagara Falls, and soon developed its own generation resources by buying private generation stations and becoming a major designer and builder of new stations. As most of the readily developed hydroelectric sites became exploited, the corporation expanded into building coal-fired generation, and then nuclear-powered facilities. Renamed as Ontario Hydro in 1974, by the 1990s it had become one of the largest, fully integrated electricity corporations in North America.

The 1970s saw increasing controversy relating to Hydro's expansion strategy, and several inquiries were held. The 1980s saw large increases in the rates charged, arising from: cost increases in the construction of the Darlington station; cost overruns for the supply of boilers by Babcock and Wilcox at the existing nuclear stations, the total for which had ballooned to $850 million; and the negotiation of take-or-pay contracts with Rio Algom and Denison Mines for the supply of uranium, prior to the collapse of world prices, which were subsequently cancelled in 1991 at a cost of $717 million. In 1998, the Legislative Assembly of Ontario passed the Energy Competition Act, 1998, which reorganized Ontario Hydro into five companies: Ontario Power Generation (OPG), the Ontario Hydro Services Company (later renamed Hydro One), the Independent Electricity Market Operator (later renamed the Independent Electricity System Operator), the Electrical Safety Authority, and Ontario Electricity Financial Corporation. The two commercial companies, Ontario Power Generation and Hydro One, were intended to eventually operate as private businesses rather than as crown corporations. The Energy Competition Act detached Ontario Hydro's $19.5 billion debt, to be paid down through a Debt Retirement Charge levied upon Ontario ratepayers. (Source: Wikipedia)

In the 1980s Ontario was still in a growth stage and there appeared to be a number of positions available in the real estate appraisal field. Some of the positions were in Ontario, and others predominantly were in the western provinces in Canada. In late 1985, one of the employers that attracted my attention was Ontario Hydro. I decided to apply for a position as a real estate appraiser and was selected for an interview at Ontario Hydro's head office at 700 University Avenue in Toronto. I was interviewed by Mr. Ken C. Crombie, Resourcing Coordinator of Ontario Hydro, and was offered the position of Contract Agent.

I accepted the position, and by way of a letter from Mr. Crombie, dated December 20, 1985, I was asked to report for my orientation meeting, complete formalities, meet certain staff at Ontario Hydro's head office on January 20 and 21, 1986, at

Ontario Hydro's Corporate Real Estate Department, and to be prepared to leave for Ottawa on January 22, 1986. By the middle of the day on January 21, 1986, a colleague (who was also hired at the same time as I was) and I were on our way to Ottawa in his car. We were instructed to report to the project office in Nepean (a suburb of Ottawa) on January 22, 1986, where we would be informed about further details of work. I arrived at the project office at 21 Concourse Gate, Nepean, on January 22, 1986. After a brief meeting with staff, a group of staff went on a tour of our assigned project, namely the St. Lawrence to Hawthorne 500 kV high voltage transmission line. That line extended from just outside Ottawa, to Cornwall. Each appraiser was assigned a number of owners in a specific location. My location in this project was the Township of Russell. The next two days, in January 1986, were spent at the Nepean project office. The week ended quickly, and by Friday January 24, 1986, my office had arranged my return trip to Toronto by an Air Canada flight.

The following week, I was allowed to drive my own car from Toronto to the Nepean project office. However, as the new hires were living in various locations in Ontario, management decided that travel by air was an efficient way to cut down on travel time and enable staff to be at the project office in the Ottawa area on Monday mornings. So I was asked to travel by air from, and to, Toronto. That meant having to take the first flight, at 6.50 am, out of Toronto International Airport on Mondays. I was allowed to fly back to Toronto, from Ottawa, on Fridays.

The weekly flights were a hectic schedule as I had to leave my home at about 4.15 am on Mondays to catch my 6.50 am flight from Toronto Pearson International Airport. Flying in the 1980s was somewhat better than conditions that existed after 9-11. The work at Ontario Hydro was interesting and the salary offered was more than I was earning at that time in the provincial government. Ontario Hydro was very accommodating to the new hires in terms of a number of allowances and training, including safety seminars and extra-curricular activities like playing curling and baseball at the local facilities in the Ottawa area. The project office had arranged a seminar at the Kemptville College of Agricultural Technology (south of Ottawa) on May 13, 1986, and a sleigh ride on February 17, 1987, which was enjoyed by all.

Based on my experiences at Ontario Hydro, in 1986, I was glad to be working there. Generally, the staff were cooperative and worked as a team. It was the best employer in comparison with my previous ones. Besides, Ottawa is a beautiful city, and, in my opinion, one of the best in Ontario. I enjoyed staying there in the 1980s. The Rideau Canal, Byward Market, historic places and buildings are just a few of the reasons that make Ottawa a wonderful place. Byward Market is a district located east of Parliament Hill and Ottawa's business district that is surrounded by George, York, Byward, and William Streets. For the most part, the property owners were pleasant to deal with, and settlements were achieved for the property rights required by Ontario Hydro. One of the major complaints of property owners, however, was the health effects of high voltage transmission lines. The owners did not want to live near such lines, or have transmission towers in their cultivated fields.

My last day at the Nepean project office was March 27, 1987. The next week, I was asked to report to Ontario Hydro's project office at 1100 Dearness Drive in London, Ontario, the location of my second project.

London is a city located in Southwestern Ontario, at the confluence of the non-navigable Thames River, approximately halfway between Toronto and Detroit, Michigan. Today, the City of London is a separated municipality, politically separate from Middlesex County, though it remains the county seat. London and the Thames were named in 1793 by Lord Simcoe, who proposed the site for the capital of Upper Canada. The first European settlement was between 1801 and 1804 by Peter Hagerman. The village was founded in 1826 and incorporated in 1855. Since then, London has grown to be the largest Southwestern Ontario municipality, having annexed many of the smaller communities that surrounded it.

London is a regional centre of health care and education, being home to the University of Western Ontario, Fanshawe College, and several hospitals. The city hosts a number of musical and artistic exhibits and festivals, which contribute to its tourism industry, but its economic activity is centred on education, medical research, insurance, and information technology. London's university and hospitals are among its top ten employers. My work for Ontario Hydro involved acquiring property rights for transmission lines in a project known as the Nanticoke Generating Station to Longwood Transformer Station 500 kV and 230 kV high voltage transmission lines.

I was responsible for the initial stage of owner contact through to appraisals, negotiations for property requirements, and settlement for damages, if any, to the owner's properties for the property rights required by Ontario Hydro in the Township of Southwold. This area had a few vocal property owners who made their views known to Ontario Hydro and the local municipality. It was a close-knit community of mainly farmers and rural residential property owners. For the most part, the offers made by Ontario Hydro to the property owners for the property requirements were fair and usually quite generous. Obviously, if a buyout by Hydro was necessary, it required the owner to move, which is where most of the disputes occurred. Obviously, when someone has to move, especially from their farming operation, or a home they have lived in for a generation or more, it is extremely upsetting to say the least. But Ontario Hydro's buyout package was usually fair, unless an owner was unable to find a suitable replacement property.

Ontario Hydro provided project staff with on-the-job training which was beneficial. One such example was a seminar on July 16, 1987, at the Agricultural College in Ridgetown. Another example is a tour of the Bruce Nuclear Station which occurred on June 18, 1987.

Various social events were also held after work, such as a lobster party on June 4, 1987, at a community facility at 790 Southdale Road (which has been converted to a park) in London, Oktoberfest in Kitchener, and the project office's Christmas party at the Seven Dwarfs Restaurant in London. There were many colleagues that I really enjoyed working with, but one of the more noteworthy ones was Ken Colmer who had a good sense of humour and was a "straight shooter." He had a sail boat named *Sea Trek*, which he personally used to sail. He reportedly took his first flight in 1951 in a single engine land and sea plane called *Tiger Moth*, when he was 18 years of age.

By mid-1989, the working conditions at Ontario Hydro had taken a turn for the worse, and various unpleasant events began to unfold. Although contract staff were switched to temporary staff, the health benefits which were proposed for the temporary staff did not materialize. Hydro required a number of permanent staff from the existing pool of temporary employees that were hired less than five years ago, around 1986. Once that quota was filled, the remaining temporary staff became expendable, that is they had to leave without any benefits.

I had applied for the permanent position, was granted an interview, and was successful at the interview; however, I was not given the position as I had indicated that I could not travel to northern Ontario on a long term basis since I required anti-nausea pills for flying. Certain staff thought that this was a result of my "fear of flying." However, they were not aware that when I was in school I wanted to be a pilot – an indication that I did not have a fear of flying.

Here's another example of the events that occurred at Hydro's project office in London in 1989. An employee at the project office would come over on several occasions near my office and stick her tongue out at me while I was working on office assignments. When I asked her why she did this, her reply was that it was her way of saying "lick my ass." A manager regarded some property agents as *plebeians*, and actually used this term on many occasions.

A supervisor greeted employees boarding an Air Canada flight by saying, "Back of the plane," when they were on board trying to find their seats on their return flight from Ottawa to Toronto. The behavior of some staff began to deteriorate to a level I had not experienced in my initial year at Ontario Hydro.

The deterioration of the office environment, not being hired for a permanent position in spite of the long hours of work and having assisted other staff with their projects at Ontario Hydro, had dehumanized me to the point that I could not work any longer at that office.

I prepared a resignation letter dated October 16, 1989, and stated my intention to resign, effective October 30, 1989. On October 24, 1989, I called the London project office and informed the receptionist that I was ill. I had a colleague return my company car and returned to my home in Mississauga by bus.

Several of the project staff informed me that they were mistreated, as will be seen in the following matters which were initiated by other colleagues and myself. The temporary employees who were not selected for a permanent position chose to seek employment elsewhere, and several left Ontario for British Columbia.

On February 18, 1992, I filed a claim in the Ontario Court (General Division) in Toronto. It was a *small claims court* claim to collect overtime while employed at Ontario Hydro, as well as for legal fees and nominal expenses of $498.78. The total amount of my claim was $1,973.07.

On March 18, 1992, Ontario Hydro disputed my claim and submitted their statement of defence and counterclaim for $2,565.65. Ontario Hydro had asked the courts that reference to the Human Rights Commission, in my small claims action against Ontario Hydro, be struck from the record, as it was a pending action. The judge, Judge D. Vanek, agreed and instructed me to also provide the defendant with particulars of the employment I had obtained subsequent to leaving Ontario Hydro. The case was to be listed for trial after August 31, 1992.

A pretrial was set for July 28, 1992, at the North York Small Claims Court, at 45 Sheppard Avenue East. The pre-trial was a method for the courts to simplify the issues and canvass the prospects of a settlement between the parties. The judge, Judge D. Vanek, asked me if I was prepared to settle if he ruled that a modest award of several hundred dollars be made by Ontario Hydro as payment to settle this matter. As I did not agree to a paltry amount being awarded to me in light of the extent of time and frustration that I had gone through over the years, the small claims matter proceeded to a hearing.

On February 22, 1993, the small claims court hearing was held at the Ontario Court (General Division) at 444 Yonge Street, 2nd floor (College Park), Toronto. Ontario Hydro was represented by their internal lawyer, who was employed by them. I represented myself for the entire process. It was winter and the GTA was experiencing a lot of snow. While consul for Ontario Hydro and their witnesses were present, I anxiously waited for some of my witnesses and was concerned that they would not appear in court in time due to a heavy snowfall. The judge indicated he was prepared to allow a postponement of the hearing in view of the prevailing weather conditions, but I decided to wait a little while longer. The wait was worth it, as all of my witnesses appeared.

At the small claims hearing, Ontario Hydro introduced an overtime summary sheet which was not submitted before the hearing, as required by law. The sheet was on legal size paper but the print was so tiny, one would have to use a magnifying glass to read it. However, I did not make an issue about it at that time, and wanted the hearing to move forward rather than be postponed. Ontario Hydro's response in their Statement of Defence included a claim for several thousand dollars as payment to hire someone else to complete my work. The judge told counsel for Ontario Hydro that they did not have to pay me, as I was no longer working there, and, instead, had to pay only the new hires, and he did not allow the claim by Ontario Hydro.

At the small claims hearing, Ontario Hydro wanted to reportedly call nineteen witnesses, whereas I had four witnesses. The judge did not want to hear any issues not directly related to the claim. However, he heard with much interest the statement made by my witness (a long-time permanent employee) pertaining to his treatment at Ontario Hydro, and the existence of an inner circle at Ontario Hydro referred to as the "Hunt Club," a close-knit group of management, and some employees, who would golf and partake in other events.

I had asked one of my witnesses to tell the court what an employee at Ontario Hydro had said to fellow staff at the project office in London in 1989, after I had left, namely that Ontario Hydro was a close-knit organization and insinuated that that could result in professional problems for me. But the judge was not interested in hearing about it, as I was not present at the time the comments were made, and the individual was not speaking to me.

The judge told Ontario Hydro that since the tenure of my employment was classified as *temporary staff,* notice of termination had to be given by them, not the other way around. Also, that I was not expected to pay the new employee for the work done by him – that was the responsibility of Ontario Hydro. If I had to serve two weeks' notice to Ontario Hydro, they would have had to pay me for that time period. In essence, the judge told Ontario Hydro that they could not claim to be reimbursed by me for the payment made to a new employee for work done by him, as I was not being paid at that time.

After the judge heard both sides, including my witnesses and what they had to say about their unfair treatment at Ontario Hydro, he dismissed the case. I chose not to appeal the case.

However, a more troublesome matter was brewing. Three other employees and I asked the Ontario Human Rights Commission to investigate the action by Hydro not to hire four single men. We retained a lawyer named Israel Balter of the legal firm of Howard Levitt & Associates in Toronto.

With respect to law, Israel Balter stated that a prima facie case of discrimination existed in our case which was never rebutted by the Commission. We had presented statistical evidence based on the results of our expert's findings and the McDonnell Douglas test.

The original case officer, Cora Tayag, an employee of the Commission who was assigned to this case, felt strongly that the issues raised by the four of us were valid, and she was prepared to hand her written report on to senior levels of the Commission. However, when the Commission found out her findings, she was reassigned to another case.

Although the new case investigator initially appeared to be sympathetic to our position, she soon held a different view which did not support our case and led us to believe she was being manipulated by senior commission staff.

In the early 1990s, the Human Rights Commission was embroiled in a $5.5 million lawsuit over allegations of racism and conspiracy within its ranks. A black manager, Glen Morrison, was fired in September 1995, for alleged mismanagement and discrimination against non-blacks. He claimed other Human Rights Commission employees fabricated charges against him. Mr. Morrison, a former Metro Toronto Police officer, had lost his house, health, and reputation after he was fired, according to his lawyer, Ernest Guiste. He was hired by the Human Rights Commission in 1981, and assigned a decade later to fix the problems at the Human Rights Commission's dysfunctional Mississauga office, where he had found the office to be plagued by a number of organizational, professional, and interpersonal problems, including racial conflict among staff.

In April 1993, our original case officer, Cora Tayag, had filed a human rights complaint against Mr. Morrison alleging discrimination on the grounds of race. The government's investigator Mark Jackson concluded Mr. Morrison had not discriminated against Ms. Tayag during a job hiring process. However, the investigator concluded that Mr. Morrison did discriminate against Cora Tayag, and other non-black staff, at work, and that a *poisoned environment based on race* pervaded

Mel H. Castelin

the Human Rights Commission office. The case by Cora Tayag was eventually settled by the Commission.

According to Howard Levitt & Associates, there is nothing in the employment arena more destructive than discrimination among applicants or employees based on their race, sex or ethnicity.

In the 1990s, the Human Rights Commission was faced with a mounting backlog of discrimination cases. In order to clear its backlog, the Commission arbitrarily began to dismiss genuine complaints of discrimination, and chose to pursue some complaints based on a narrow ideologically driven agenda.

Three cases were noted by Howard Levitt, a Toronto-based employment lawyer: Case 1 was an employer who announced that all females of child-bearing age would be demoted in favour of older, more career-oriented women; Case 2 was where an employer introduced practices favouring married males over single ones for promotions to permanent jobs; Case 3 was a customer who complained that a variety store was selling adult magazines which objectified women.

Most people would agree that the first and second cases, if substantiated, would involve discrimination based on age, sex, or marital status, and violated the Human Rights Code. By contrast, Case 3 has nothing to do with discrimination, as the complainant was not denied a job or service because of her sex. The Human Rights Commission, however, had a different view. It declined to investigate Case 1 or Case 2, and proceeded to vigorously prosecute a family-owned variety store for selling adult magazines such as *Playboy*.

It was common for Ontario Hydro staff to sponsor golfing and other events. In fact, one such person that had helped organize many events in the Real Estate & Security Division of Ontario Hydro was Crissy Munro, whose family reportedly had political affiliations with the Liberal party. She was on friendly terms with certain management in Ontario Hydro's project office, and would reportedly snitch on employees. Initially, she too was classified as a temporary employee, but she was later hired as a permanent employee, even though many employees in the project office had to complete the work she had been assigned.

The serious problems at Hydro were *top down*, namely they originated at senior levels. In fact, by the 1990s, the Ombudsman warned that the Ontario civil service was in a crisis situation. Over the years, the media had extensively commented on the boondoggle that existed at Ontario Hydro.

On September 25, 1992, the Board of Directors of Ontario Hydro had reportedly voted 8 to 5 to ask Ontario Hydro's President Al Holt to take early retirement, thereby ending his 36-year career at the age of 60 years. Mr. Holt was in Madrid attending the afternoon session of the World Energy Conference when he received a call from Larry Leonoff, Ontario Hydro's general counsel. Premier Bob Rae's NDP appointees to the Board of Directors of Ontario Hydro had sealed Mr. Holt's fate.

Mr. Holt was precluded from talking about his firing, as he was required to sign a non-disclosure agreement in lieu of the compensation package offered to him, which was reported to be a very significant amount.

The firing of Mr. Holt was reportedly the outcome of a dirty, ideological war that began about 15 months earlier when Mr. Marc Eliesen was appointed Chairman of Ontario Hydro at a reported salary of $325,000 a year, which was going to be raised to $400,000 a year; but, later he was forced to take a pay cut of $260,000 a year. Mr. Eliesen was reported to be a backroom worker for the NDP at the federal and provincial levels. Mr. Eliesen had wanted the chairmanship position, as well as that of president and chief operating officer; but, the board of directors did not consider Mr. Eliesen worthy of both positions, and hired Mr. Holt as president.

On October 5, 1992, the Energy Minister, Mr. Brian Charlton, told the Legislature that he was not aware of Al Holt's firing until four days after the fact. Furthermore, Mr. Charlton claimed he was not aware that Mr. Holt had been fired, and his understanding was that Mr. Holt had resigned. The firing of Al Holt was the first in a series of moves that culminated with the appointment of Maurice Strong as Ontario Hydro's new Chairman. Employee morale at Ontario Hydro during that time was at an all-time low for the reported 28,600 employees, for mainly two reasons: One is that there had been a 20% hydro rate increase over the previous two years at the time of a severe recession; and secondly, up to 2,000 jobs at Ontario Hydro were to be eliminated in a move to downsize Ontario Hydro.

But, the most important reason for the turmoil at Ontario Hydro was a clash between the anti-nuclear and pro-conservation government, and Ontario Hydro's long-ensconced pro-nuclear establishment.

In the early 1990s, the Chairman of Ontario Hydro was Maurice Strong. His business arrangements had been so complicated that they were sure to make one's head spin. Strong's deals reportedly involved U.S. oil interests, Saudi arms merchant Adnan Kashoggi, Canada's Power Corp., and the man who was federal Finance Minister, Paul Martin.

Maurice Strong was an employee of the Rockefeller and Rothschild's trusts and projects, a director of the Aspen Institute for Humanistic Studies, the organizer of the first World Conference on the Environment in Rio de Janeiro in June 1992, the founder and first head of the U.N. Environment Program, the secretary general (and chief organizer) of the UNCED Earth Summit in Rio in June 1992, and a leading socialist, environmentalist, New World Order manipulator, occultist, and New Ager. In the mid-1980s, Strong joined the World Commission on the Environment where he helped produce the 1987 Brundtland Report, widely believed to be the "incendiary" which ignited the present *Green movement.*

In 1971, Maurice Strong commissioned a report on the state of the planet called, *Only One Earth: The Care and Maintenance of a Small Planet,* co-authored by Barbara Ward and Rene Dubos. It led to the establishment by the UN General Assembly in December 1972, of the United Nations Environment Program (UNEP), with headquarters in Nairobi, Kenya, and the election of Maurice Strong to head it.

In 1976, at the request of Prime Minister Pierre Trudeau, Maurice Strong returned to Canada to head the newly created national oil company, Petro-Canada. It should not have surprised anybody, when years later, Strong became the architect of the multi-billion dollar Kyoto Protocol. Strong, who spearheaded the Earth Summit, had complained that "the United States was clearly the greatest risk to the world's ecological health," and wrote in an UNCED report in August 1991, that: "It is clear that current lifestyles and consumption patterns of the affluent middle-class . . . involving high meat intake, consumption of large amounts of frozen and convenience foods, ownership of motor vehicles, small electric appliances, home and work place air-conditioning, and suburban housing are not sustainable . . . A shift is necessary toward life-styles less geared to environmental damaging consumption patterns." Maurice Strong had forcefully advocated a new economic order based on the re-distribution of the developed world's industries and wealth to the Third World. Strong appeared to be an arch socialist.

The Trilateral Commission had published a book, *Beyond Interdependence: The Meshing of the World's Economy and the Earth's Ecology.* Rockefeller wrote the foreword and Maurice Strong wrote the introduction, saying in part: "This book couldn't appear at a better time, with the preparation for the Earth Summit moving into gear . . . it will help guide decisions that will literally determine the fate of the earth . . . Rio will have the political capacity to produce the basic changes needed in our international economic agendas and in our institutions of governance."

Maurice Strong had established what could be the global headquarters for the New Age movement, in the San Luis Valley of Colorado, at the foot of the Sangre de Cristo Mountains, near Crestone, Colorado. He and his wife Hanne who has been described to be *occultic*, referred to the Baca Centre as an international spiritual community, which they hoped would serve as a model for the way the world should be if humankind is to survive – a sort of United Nations of religious beliefs. The Baca was replete with monasteries: the Haidakhrndi Universal Ashram, a Vedic temple where devotees worshiped the Vedic mother goddess; amulet-carrying Native American shamans; a $175,000 solar-powered Hindu temple; a mustard-yellow tower called a ziggurat; a subterranean Zen Buddhist center, complete with a computer and organic gardens; a house full of thousands of crystals; and even Shirley MacLaine and her New Age followers. In 1978, it was reported a mystic informed Hanne and Maurice Strong that "the Baca would become the center for a new planetary order which would evolve from the economic collapse and environmental catastrophes that would sweep the globe in the years to come." The Strong's considered the Baca, which they called *The Valley of the Refuge of World Truths*, as the paradigm for the entire planet, and were of the opinion that the fate of the earth was at stake. Reportedly, Shirley MacLaine agreed – her astrologer had told her to move to the Baca, and she did. She built a New Age study center at the Baca where people took short week-long courses on the occult. Apparently, the Kissinger's, the Rockefeller's, the McNamara's, the Rothschild's, and other Establishment New World Order elitists all agreed as well, for they did their pilgrimage to the Baca, where politics and the occult – the New World Order and the New Age – all merged.

Maurice Strong was far and away the most effective executive that Ontario Hydro had ever had. Within a short time of his arrival, he firmly redirected and re-structured Ontario Hydro. At the time, Ontario Hydro was hell-bent on building many more nuclear reactors, despite dropping demand and rising prices. Maurice Strong grabbed the Corporation by the scruff of the neck, reduced the workforce by one third, stopped the nuclear expansion plans, cut capital expenditures, froze the price of electricity, pushed for sustainable development, and made business units more accountable.

But in 1992, miles away, Costa Rica's Ministry of Natural Resources filed charges against Maurice Strong and his partner in Desarollos Ecologicos S.A., for building their $35 million, 12-unit Villas del Caribe on land located in the Kekoldi Indian Reserve, and Gandoca-Manzanillo Wildlife Refuge, without official permits. According to Demetrio Myorga, President of the Kekoldi Indian Association, Maurice Strong was supporting Indians and conservation around the world, and in Costa Rica he was doing the complete opposite.

Mel H. Castelin

Back in 1994, Ontario Hydro Chairman, Maurice Strong, opened talks on buying 12,500 hectares (30,875 acres) of a Costa Rican forest in the face of the utility's then $34 billion debt.

Strong, a Special Advisor to the Secretary General of the United Nations, and President of the United Nations University for Peace in Costa Rica, was appointed to Ontario Hydro by former Ontario Premier Bob Rae, who remembered him as a friend of his father's and called him "Uncle Moe." Uncle Moe got around, and, before joining Ontario Hydro, he had served as President, Chairman and Chief Executive Officer of Petro Canada, and earlier as President of Power Corporation of Canada.

Paul Desmarais was chairman of Power Corporation. Prime Minister Jean Chretien's daughter France, is married to Andre Desmarais, son of Paul Desmarais. Ex-Conservative Prime Minister Brian Mulroney has been a lawyer and lobbyist for Power Corporation, which, together with Ontario Hydro and Hydro Quebec, formed the Hong-Kong-based ASIA Power Corp., to help China to develop its energy potential.

Ontario Hydro had been in the news a lot in the 1980s and 1990s, mostly being criticized by its many detractors. Criticism reached a peak as Maurice Strong was being recruited as Chairman in the early 1990s. Much of this criticism was valid: electricity prices were rising; construction costs were spiraling; management wanted to continue overbuilding nuclear reactors; and the Corporation was not exactly user-friendly. Ontario Hydro was also well-known for its impenetrable bureaucracy. Maurice Strong changed the Corporation's direction radically: new reactor plans were canned; one third of the labour force was cut; Management was (nominally) made more responsible; emphasis shifted from nuclear to sustainable development; electricity prices were frozen. By the 1990s, the Corporation was in much better financial shape as debt was declining; profits rising (except for abnormal items); and prices frozen. However, the large nuclear program was still limping. Nuclear had dropped to 47% of the province's electricity supply, down from 60% a few years earlier. Hydro had hired a group of seven Americans to run the Nuclear Division, which appeared to show positive results.

On April 1, 1999, Chairman, Bill Farlinger, announced the division of the old Ontario Hydro into five new companies. The guts of Ontario Hydro was the generation capacity, mainly nuclear. The Transmission and Distribution and the other portions could be easily split off. However, the new Ontario Power still had 90% of the generation capacity in the Province, and there were few connections to Quebec, Manitoba, Michigan, etc., so nobody could really sell in. It was just a natural monopoly – no real changes to the company, no changes in people or the bureaucracy, probably little competition; this restructuring was regarded as a con job. Ontario Hydro's Stalinsque bureaucracy had remained in place, despite the "re-structuring" that had occurred in the 1990s.

In 1992, an employee at Ontario Hydro, Michael Moles, Ph.D., M.B.A., P.Eng. (Senior Scientist – NDE, Advanced Systems Technology, Ontario Hydro Technologies) alleged fraud and corruption at the top levels of Ontario Hydro in the mid-nineties. Following his allegations of fraud in Ontario Hydro Technologies in 1992, Ontario Hydro Management called in their Internal Audit, and reportedly covered up the fraud. Moles hired top Private Investigators to produce a *one-step short of criminal fraud* case, which they did very well. Ontario Hydro hired Arthur Anderson to investigate his new allegations, then apparently forged Arthur Anderson's report. Ontario Hydro fired Moles for insubordination in November 1996, but his union (The Society of Ontario Hydro Professional and Administrative Employees) had held onto the case, and they obviously didn't want this news out either. He suspected the Arthur Anderson report was a forgery because all Arthur Anderson reports have the authors' names on the top or bottom of the report, signatures, and report numbers. That report did not. The content was also faulty; the report claimed to investigate the Hydro Internal Audit (IA) report, but didn't check the financial figures. For example, the Hydro Internal Audit should have listed all purchase orders, and the IA report did not. Who had been involved in Hydro-gate? It was reported to be the ex-Senior Legal Council (Larry Leonoff), the ex-Chairman (Maurice Strong), and a number of other top-level Hydro managers, plus lower level employees. Many of those involved still worked for Hydro, including the focus of Michael Moles' initial investigation, Jim Brown.

The issues raised by Mr. Michael Moles corroborates the working conditions experienced by me and others within Ontario Hydro.

The Conservative government of Premier Mike Harris was embarrassed at the manner in which business was being conducted in Ontario Hydro in the 1990s. An article in the June 1999 issue of *Report On Business* magazine outlined details of some salaries and consultants fees paid by the utility to friends of the conservative government.

In 2002, Eleanor Clitheroe was CEO and president of Hydro One. However, the media reported there was a level of corporate greed that was represented by Eleanor Clitheroe's negotiated compensation package, and sanctioned by a complacent board of directors, which showed just how far out of touch with the average person Hydro One and the corporate community had become. Hydro One had sponsored a racing yacht called *Defiant* for $360,000 over three years. In 2001, Eleanor Clitheroe, an avid sailor, had received $2.2 million in compensation, including a salary of $750,000, a bonus of $806,250, a car allowance of $174,644, and other allowances of $451,286, which included a vacation allowance of $172,484. In 2002, she negotiated a $6 million severance clause and a pension package that was to pay as much as $1 million a year for life. The former Premier Ernie Eves government had passed the Hydro One Directors and Officers Act which was an attempt to limit executive compensation. On July 19, 2002, Clitheroe was fired, and Hydro One alleged, due to her abuses of power, she would not get the $6 million severance package. It is interesting to note that Eleanor Clitheroe had a privatization plan for Hydro One. In June 2002, Hydro One's entire board of directors resigned in protest after the provincial government moved to fire them and roll back executive salaries. Eleanor Clitheroe became an Anglican cleric.

Fast forward to 2015:

The sale of Hydro One crystalized in 2015. But the framework for change within the Corporation was well underway before then. The insiders knew that big change was coming to the Corporation.

But it is interesting to note that while Hydro One elected to make drastic cutbacks, executives at the Corporation, at the same time, enriched themselves with significantly large compensation packages.

The Canadian Taxpayers Federation (CTF) blamed Ontario's Liberal government and the cost of their gas plant cancellations for electricity rate increases that came into effect. The price for off-peak power had increased by 7.5 per cent per kilowatt-hour, while peak hour rates had risen by 4 per cent. Both increases were significantly higher than the rate of inflation. According to Candice Malcolm, Ontario Director of the CTF, "This might as well be called the 'Gas Plant Scandal Tax'. We now know that electricity ratepayers are on the hook to pay for the cancelled plants, so it was just a matter of time before rates were hiked once again." "We're paying for this government's incompetence, vote-buying, and their utter mismanagement of the energy file in Ontario," according to Candice Malcolm. "From their costly and ill-conceived Green Energy Act, which pays wind farms not to produce energy, and offers a billion-dollar-a-year subsidy to hide green energy rate increases known as the Ontario Clean Energy Benefit, to paying TransCanada not to build a gas plant, this government is demonstrating sheer incompetency in energy," concluded Candice Malcolm.

The Auditor General report on the cancelled gas plants shows that the cost for the political decisions made during the last provincial election, add up to $1.1 billion. The remainder of this cost will be paid for by electricity ratepayers over the next 20 years.

Summary

There was an unusual turn of events that occurred during the fourth year of my employment. I was not hired for a permanent position, as I had disclosed at my interview that I was unable to fly to northern Ontario on a long term basis due to a need for medication for flying. Management used my disclosure to deny me a permanent position. Yet, when questioned about this by the judge in small claims court, Hydro took the position that I threatened to quit, which was a blatant lie, as it was Ontario Hydro who threatened me by asking me to choose between travelling to northern Ontario or having to apply for a position elsewhere. In hindsight, by Ontario Hydro wanting me to travel to northern Ontario, knowing I had a health issue with flying, amounted to a breach of the Human Rights Code and constructive termination, for which I should have received appropriate compensation.

The work environment began to change soon after Ontario Hydro had accomplished its project objectives of acquisition of the requirements for the high voltage transmission lines in eastern and southwestern Ontario. In addition, due to budgetary constraints, a broad range of cutbacks occurred, which included staff. It is interesting to note that while the cutbacks took place, the level of corporate greed continued at Ontario Hydro, resulting in huge salary payments and payouts at the corporate level.

A study of working relationships in Ontario Hydro was initiated by management as a consequence of an increased level of concern at the senior executive level that working relationships in the Union, The Society of Ontario Hydro Professional & Administrative Employees and various employee groups were in need of improvement. This resulted in a study being published in April 1986, by Ferris Associates and Halpern Associates Inc., which contained its findings, underlying causes, management initiatives and recommendations. It stated that there were management practices and behaviours that were adversely affecting working relationships, and the Human Resources Branch needed to be a stronger advocate of enlightened human resource management. (Source: A Study of Working Relationships in Ontario Hydro, published April 1986, by Ferris Associates and Halpern Associates Inc.)

Finally, it is worth noting that in the 1970s, Ontario Hydro gave Denison Mines, a mining company owned by Stephen Roman, a 31-year sweetheart uranium deal said to be worth $7.3 billion, including a $340 million interest-free loan with no cancellation until the early 1990s, and a guaranteed undisclosed price for the uranium. One estimate indicated it would yield Denison Mines a windfall profit of a bare minimum of $1.6 billion.

Until 1991, I had worked for provincial or municipal governments. But, in the next chapter, you are going to read about my first venture for work in the private sector, with a real estate appraisal and planning firm.

Sources: *The Toronto Star*, June 5, 2002, June 8, 2002, July 20, 2002, December 24, 2010; An article by Michael Moles was first published May 23, 1999; the contents of the web site represent opinions of Michael Moles; *Controlling Interest* by Diane Francis – Macmillan of Canada, October 1986; *On the Way to Parliament: Uncle Mo in Activist Mode* by Judi McLeod, *Canada Free Press*, September 1, 2003; Maurice Strong and The New World Order Intelligence Update – www.gwb.com.au; Toward A New World Order by Donald McAlvany – Hearthstone Publishing, October 1990

CHAPTER 4

My Employment for 23 Years
in the Private Sector

One day, in September 1991, the principal of gsi Real Estate & Planning Advisors Inc. called me to see if I would be interested in joining him to set-up an appraisal company. At the time I was employed with a regional municipality in Ontario. As I had known the principal for many years, the opportunity of working in the private sector was appealing to me, at the time.

Working at gsi enabled me to prepare appraisal reports on projects, mostly in the Greater Toronto Area, on behalf of many of the major law firms, numerous municipalities, development corporations, major banks, colleges, universities, school boards, provincial government, several municipal governments, and Canadian National.

My particular area of expertise was in real estate appraisal for individual properties and large-scale projects, including partial takings of various types of properties that were expropriated by Expropriating Authorities in Ontario. I worked well with the private sector, small and large law firms, and governmental agencies in Ontario. I provided valuable expertise for complex appraisal assignments involving real estate litigation. For twenty-three years, I prepared hundreds of appraisal reports of sites for commercial, industrial, residential, agricultural, waterfront, rural, special-use, high-density residential development, and subdivision lands, in various areas of the Province of Ontario. My reports resulted in a high number of settlements.

Some of the major projects I worked on included the following:

- Regional Municipality of York's H3 Viva Rapid Transit Project, along a dedicated corridor of Regional Road 7 (Highway 7), in Richmond Hill and Markham
- York Region's Y1 Rapid Transit Project, along Yonge Street in Vaughan and Markham, for VIVAs proposed subway system
- Valuation of West Don Lands, City of Toronto
- Appraisal of various properties for the Toronto Police, for possible mortgage fraud
- Appraisal of Riverdale Hospital, Toronto, for its redevelopment with a new hospital complex, now operating as Bridgepoint Health
- Appraisals for Easton Group of Companies of a site at Dundas Street East/Jarvis Street, for a Comfort Inn Hotel; Comfort Inn & restaurant complex in Port Hope; and Comfort Inn in Peterborough

An interesting project I appraised was a complex of commercial properties near Ontario Street and Highway 401 in Port Hope, which was owned by Steve Gupta, now president and chief executive officer of Easton's Group of Hotels Inc. Port Hope is a municipality in Southern Ontario, about 109 km east of Toronto. It is located at the mouth of the Ganaraska River, on the north shore of Lake Ontario, in the west end of Northumberland County.

My assignment in Port Hope was comprised of a truck stop, card lock, gas bar, Harvey's, Church's Chicken, and a Comfort

Inn Hotel. It is reported that Steve Gupta had acquired the original development of a truck stop and gas bar in Port Hope in 1978, when he had saved up enough money, by selling insurance, to make his first real estate acquisition. He walked in and put everything he had, namely a mere $15,000 in cash, into the $3 million deal.

The other appraisal assignment that I worked on for Steve Gupta was the site of the former Royal Canadian Mounted Police (RCMP) office building at 200 Dundas Street East and Jarvis Street, which was redeveloped with a Comfort Inn Hotel. The assignment was essentially an Income Approach, more specifically a discounted cash flow analysis where the projected income stream of the proposed Comfort Inn was analyzed. Although I completed the appraisal report, and Mr. Gupta obtained financing for the project, which was subsequently constructed, I was doubtful of the success of the hotel project because of the proximity of a strip bar across the street, and the down-trodden characteristics of the area. But, a few years later, the area had slowly transformed, with many new developments. According to Steve Gupta, money and happiness are not the same thing, as money cannot buy health, happiness, or success. He believes success means doings things that are valuable to him, his family, and the community.

One day, a client, Bill Assaf, walked into our office with a request for an appraisal of a property at 140 Dunvegan Road in Forest Hill, which he claimed was a matter of litigation. He was willing to retain gsi, and, for a retainer, he rolled up his trouser and removed ten $100 bills from his sock – I still cannot forget that day. He had a cheque delivered for another thousand dollars, but he did not pay the balance of my appraisal fees, which amounted to over $5,000 for the appraisal of three properties.

The 140 Dunvegan Road property had been the subject of legal battles, dating back to the 1971 death of Edward Assaf, and a will that left only small annual amounts to his son, Bill. For more than four decades, and through 30 lawsuits, *litigious warfare* was waged for the Forest Hill mansion. The dispute dates back to the 1971 death of Edward Assaf, who left his substantial estate to his daughter, and only small annual payments for his son and estranged wife, the late Vivian Assaf. Since that time, the son and wife have unsuccessfully sued: Robert Bosada, the executor of Edward Assaf's estate (and the junior Assaf's uncle); Bosada's lawyer, Bernard Burton; and the owners of Assaf's former home, Mary Matthews and James Archer-Shee, who stumbled into the Assaf family maelstrom. The pair bought the home in 1998 for $1.4 million and have faced several court battles since. In his March 6, 2013 ruling, Justice E.M. Morgan threw out the latest in a long line of claims by Bill Assaf to regain ownership of his father's Forest Hill home. The judge branded Bill Assaf a *vexatious litigant*, after a *long and bitter vendetta* in the courts with everyone involved in his father's estate. In a ruling strewn with indictments of the perpetual plaintiff, William Assaf, Justice Morgan attempted to finally end what he called *Ontario's longest running legal drama,* that, even 30 years ago, was described by another judge as a *long and bitter vendetta* against the estate of Assaf's father, Edward, and "everyone that touches it."

There were numerous other cases involving the *Assaf* family. In an earlier case, Bill Assaf attempted to bring forward another will that he claimed his father wrote. It was ruled a forgery, and Bill Assaf was sentenced to four years in penitentiary, which was later reduced to two and a half years. Bosada, Edward Assaf's executor, was also found to have forged a document, but a judge ultimately found that it had no bearing on the ownership of the property. During the 40-year period of the lawsuits, judges have commented on the destructive nature of the continual cases.

A view of the house at 140 Dunvegan Road, Forest Hill

One judge noted the litigants from the family were "figures in a classical tragedy, bent upon destroying that which surrounds them and especially their monetary inheritance." According to Daniel Barna, William Assaf's agent, Bill Assaf was going to appeal the decision and had drafted a notice of claim to be filed. (Source: Wendy Gillis, *Toronto Star,* March 19, 2013)

I was asked to appraise a property on the south side of Beaumont Road in one of the most expensive residential areas of Toronto, known as Rosedale. The objective of the appraisal report was to establish the market value of the property, taking into consideration the fact that a few houses were already established on the south side of Beaumont Road, which were built some 20 feet to 50 feet down from the road into a ravine leading to the Don Valley. During my research, I uncovered a sale of a home on the north side of Beaumont Road, namely 5 Beaumont Road, which had been owned and occupied by the well-known singer, Gordon Lightfoot. He sold the property a number of years ago for a few million; since that time, house values have gone up considerably in the area. The mansion at the very end of Beaumont Road was lived in by a former Archbishop of Toronto, and reportedly sold when the archbishop passed away.

My appraisal assignments included unique types of properties, including the former Riverdale Hospital (now Bridgepoint Health) for its redevelopment. It is situated within the north-west quadrant of Gerrard Street East and Coxwell Avenue, in the Riverdale community of Toronto. Riverdale Hospital first opened its doors in 1860, as the first Toronto shelter for the homeless. Just over a decade later, the space was converted to help contain the 1869 smallpox epidemic. Over the next 50 years, it developed a reputation for treating infectious diseases, and housed patients suffering from the illnesses of the day, including diphtheria, scarlet fever, tuberculosis, measles, and polio. This hospital continued to evolve with the community needs by opening a stroke recovery unit, a palliative care unit, a dialysis unit, and an HIV/AIDS complex continuing care program. Bridgepoint Health constructed a 464-bed rehabilitation and complex care hospital, the single largest organization in Canada to focus exclusively on research, care, and teaching, for people with complex health conditions. It is situated next to the former Don Jail which was completed in 1864, and recently renovated to serve as the administrative wing of Bridgepoint Health.

Another project included the valuation of lengthy CN railway corridors for their sale to Metrolinx. It is interesting to note that Metrolinx was acquiring lands in downtown Toronto at a time when land prices had escalated to an all-time high and most of downtown Toronto was built-out, or many areas adjacent to the CN railway corridor were being developed with high density condominium buildings. The government allowed immigration but did not plan for it by ensuring there was adequate mass transit in place before the significant influx of people, or commuters, to downtown Toronto.

An example of the unfairness of an expropriating authority is illustrated in the expropriation by the Ministry of Transportation from a property owner in the Municipality of Shuniah, east of Thunder Bay. The Ministry of Transportation required a portion of the owner's large residential holding for a twinning of a new section of Highway 11/17. It was prepared to compensate the owner for the market value of only the required land but not for injurious affection or the loss in market value to the remainder, which is compensable under the regulations of the Expropriations Act – the regulation of the provincial government that governs how an expropriated property owner is compensated.

The MTO requirement created a severance of the northern 51.97 acres and left the balance of the remainder fronting on the old Highway 11/17, which served as a local municipal road. In order to access their northern severed parcel on the new Highway 11/17, the subject owners had the inconvenience of travelling over two kilometres easterly on the said local road (old Highway 11/17), to Birch Beach Road, and then had to travel westerly to the northern severed parcel. In order to get back home, the owners had to travel west on the new Highway 11/17 to MacKenzie Heights Road, and southerly along the said road, and easterly along the old highway 11/17, to their home. The MTO indicated that it was prepared to allow the subject owners a private access to the northern remainder parcel from a private road known as Shuniah Forest Products Road, which extends to Highway 11/17. No other access, from or crossing over the new highway, was allowed.

Access to Shuniah Forest Products Road, on the south side of the new highway, was to be closed. Consequently, the owners had to trailer their ATV or snowmobile in order to access the northern remainder lands. The new highway would be a divided highway, and contain four lanes.

My opinion of the effect of the requirement expropriated by MTO was as follows:

A loss of land area of about 11.07 acres; a loss of trees (merchantable timber value or firewood value); the creation of a severance of about 51.97 acres to the north and inconvenience of getting to it, resulting in its diminution in value; the residence on the southern remainder would be sandwiched between the old and new highway; a loss of the future potential for development of a portion of the existing highway frontage for highway commercial use; the inconvenience of having to travel about 2.5 km along old Highway 11/17 (which would be a local road) to get to the new Highway 11/17 via Birch Beach Road; a greater distance and travel time for emergency vehicles to get to the subject property; an increase in noise levels as the subject property would have a new highway to the north and a local road to the south; an increase in pollution; a potential impact on the future marketability of the property; a loss of utility; a loss of quiet enjoyment; a perceived and measurable loss in market value of the subject property; and a general nuisance and associated costs during construction of the highway.

The above is an example of how very unfair a government department can be to a property owner in view of a loss sustained to a property by an expropriation. In many instances this provincial government department chose not to compensate property owners fairly, which resulted in a lengthy waiting period and added legal and other costs.

Generally, the approach taken by the government is to compensate a property owner for the land expropriated, with the owner having to prove if there is a loss in value or injurious affection sustained to a property.

My appraisal experience included the preparation of appraisals of special use properties such as golf courses, railway corridors, service stations and hotels. A special use property that was appraised by me was Whitby Psychiatric Hospital, in Whitby, Ontario, previously known as Ontario Hospital for the Insane, a mental health facility. The original facility was replaced in 1996 by a modern hospital that currently operates under the name of Ontario Shores Centre for Mental Health Sciences. In 1911, the Government of Ontario announced that a new *asylum* would be built to replace a similar facility in Toronto, and a 624-acre (253 hectares) site on Lake Ontario, in Whitby, was selected the following year. Whitby was chosen due its relative proximity to Toronto, and for cheap power and water provided by local utilities. Most of the buildings of the new Ontario Hospital for the Insane were constructed from 1913 to 1916. Upon completion, the site was taken over by the Government of Canada to serve as a military convalescent hospital for soldiers wounded in the First World War. The facility was returned to the Ontario government in 1919.

The hospital was considered a model of mental health care for its era. Patients were housed in a cottage setting in an attempt to provide a home-like atmosphere to those undergoing treatment. The lakeside, fresh air environment was also seen as beneficial, as was the attached hospital farm. The farm was intended to make the facility self-sufficient in meat, milk, and vegetables, and it operated until 1969. At its peak, the hospital was home to 1,650 patients. However, starting in the 1950s, new advancements in medication, therapy, and care, enabled a greater degree of community care. In 1968, the name of the facility was changed to the Whitby Psychiatric Hospital. As more patients were discharged into community settings, the number of in-patients dropped from 1,000 to 504, between 1970 and 1977. A nursing school was operated on the site from 1920 to 1972, when the responsibility for nursing training was transferred to Ontario's colleges.

THE FRONT ENTRANCE TO ONTARIO SHORES CENTRE FOR MENTAL HEALTH SCIENCES

This property was appraised by me based on its existing use, which resulted in an application of the Cost Approach to value, namely an estimate of the depreciated reproduction cost of the improvements and the market value of the land. I retained a cost consultant to provide a building cost estimate. Inspection of the facility took a significant amount of time. I was not permitted to view certain areas of the building due to privacy rules for the in-patients. But my walk along the southern section of the property offered a spectacular view of Lake Ontario and the property. In 1979, provincial studies indicated that the facility should be rebuilt. Construction on the new hospital began several years later in 1993, and was officially opened as the Whitby Mental Health Centre, in 1996. (Sources: Wikipedia; Ontario Shores Centre For Mental Health Sciences)

Summary

The appraisal of institutional or government real property assets can be, in some instances, more complex than non-institutional assets.

My comprehensive valuations were presented in detailed and transparent reports, and often resulted in immediate *buy-in* among participating parties concerning the value opined, which resulted in an efficient and timely acquisition/disposition of the properties in many public sector projects. They translated into successful outcomes for the clients of projects such as the Whitby Psychiatric Hospital, Bridgepoint Health, and the Regional Municipality of York, to achieve a high number of settlements for their Highway 7 VIVA Project.

Generally, the gsi clients were reasonable in terms of the compensation they expected for their properties. It was my function to estimate the market value of a property and substantiate the basis of the compensation. The Expropriations Act provided a property owner to receive market value and injurious affection, or loss in value, to the remainder, as a result of an expropriation. It was legitimate for an appraiser to ignore the scheme, or purpose, of the property owner's land in determining the market value of a property, before the existence of the expropriation. There were some instances where property owners were unreasonable and expected more than what could be justified.

By 2013, I had worked exclusively for gsi for 23 years, which was the longest period of time I had worked for one employer.

It is essential for an employment contract to exist between an employee and employer prior to an employee commencing work for a company. Where an employment contract has been signed by an employee, the terms of that contract would apply. However, in the absence of an employment contract, common law applies in Ontario. In the case of a termination, the law would consider a person's age, length of employment, and one's position in that company. This applies to large and small companies. An employment lawyer is the best source of information, if you should have any doubts.

While I was working at Ontario Hydro, I encountered a number of really challenging issues outside the workplace which I had to deal with on weekends. They are discussed in the next chapter, and I am sure that they would amaze anyone.

CHAPTER 5

My Ordeal Purchasing Condos and Being a Landlord

A proposed condominium project known as *BloorEast* in downtown Toronto

My business partner, Bill Proskos, was the owner of a limousine company called Manhattan Limousine Service Inc., in Toronto. He was one of the first limo owners in Toronto to offer the public the booking of a limo car with gull-wing doors, in addition to a Bentley, stretch Lincoln Continental, and Mercedes Benz. He struck me as being an entrepreneur who wanted to be different from the competition. He had a sense of humour and was pleasant to talk to.

I met Bill Proskos after I called his company to book a limousine to get me from my home to Toronto airport. As I liked the service his company provided, I decided to call his company for my business trips on Mondays to Toronto Pearson International Airport.

In a short time, Bill and I were talking about real estate, and he seemed keen on investing in real estate. We decided to jointly purchase a condominium unit in a downtown Toronto project, and determined that a good location to invest in was along Bloor Street. One proposed condominium building advertisement that caught our eye was BloorEast, at 400 Bloor Street East, the second property west of Sherbourne Street; a bank occupied the north west corner of that intersection. The developer of BloorEast was Hersh Fogel; Jack Diamond was the architect, Martin Atkins was the marketer and Bob Forrest & Bryon Patton were the space planners. Jack Diamond has designed award-winning buildings in Canada and around the world, including exclusive houses, major health care centres, and the Toronto Opera House, for the Canadian Opera Company. A glimpse of the key players in BloorEast is visible on the next page.

On October 3, 1986, I viewed the *BloorEast* condo project in their sales office at 387 Bloor Street East, Toronto, and spoke with Molly Silverstein, the sales representative, in order to obtain the project details. After reviewing the project details, and talking to a number of people, I felt the project was a good one, and Bill Proskos and I signed an agreement of purchase and sale on October 11, 1986, to purchase Suite 904, in *BloorEast*, for $213,900. The said agreement was accepted by the developer's company, Guided Investments Limited, on October 17, 1986. Our total down payment was $21,390. The transaction was to be completed on June 1, 1988, which was a reasonable time frame for construction of the proposed building. The unit had two bedrooms, a den, two washrooms, and high quality finishes, with an area of 1,200 sq. ft. It was a north-facing, corner unit, with a gorgeous view of Rosedale ravine.

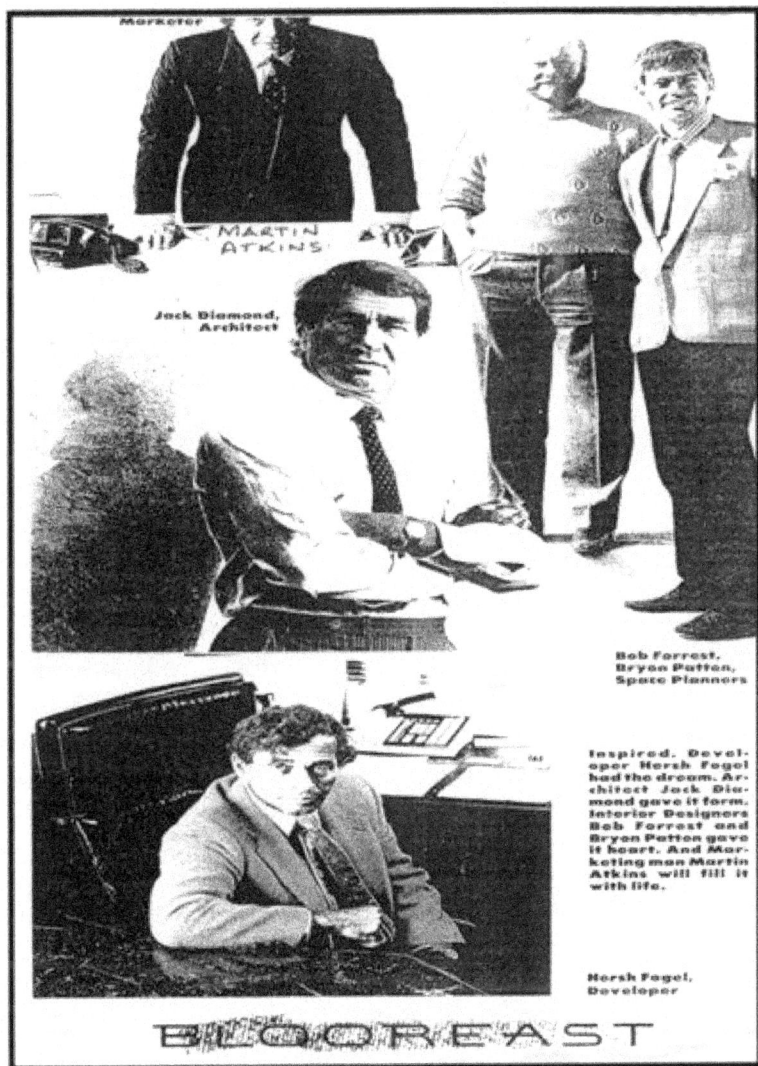

Five of the key people of the proposed
BloorEast condominium development

The developer's company, responsible for constructing the proposed 75-unit condominium apartment building, was Guided Investments Limited, which was part of the Guided Group, with their office at 66 Guided Court, Rexdale (Etobicoke), Ontario. Their Vice-President of real estate development was Mr. Howard Dixon.

The developer had indicated that the proposed building would be constructed by the summer of 1988. In 1987, I made numerous calls to the sales office on Bloor Street East to ascertain the timing of completion of the proposed condominium building. The sales office took the position that the building would be ready as indicated in our agreement. However, many months went by and I anxiously waited to hear about the progress of the proposed project.

I had ascertained that the developer had not obtained municipal approval, which was of concern to all of the purchasers in this development. One of the unresolved issues was the access point for construction equipment, namely if construction access was to be approved from Bloor Street East, or from the other end of the site, namely Rosedale Valley Road.

There were a number of issues, including the fact that the developer had not received a building permit from the City of Toronto to construct the proposed condominium building, although they had applied for one in November 1988, which was well past the date of construction of the building indicated in our Agreement of Purchase and Sale. Consequently, the developer encountered cost over-runs of the project. We, and many of the other purchasers, had difficulty in getting a response regarding the completion date of the project from the developer, more specifically Mr. Howard Dixon of Guided Investments Limited.

We heard through reliable sources that the developer was having difficulty commencing the project at the original cost estimate and was attempting to shelve the development. If the developer was able to cancel the project by returning the deposit moneys to the purchaser's, or disqualifying bona fide purchaser's, they could start a new project at unit prices considerably higher than that originally offered to the public, or they could sell the land to another developer for a much higher price, as the market value of residential development land had reached an all-time high in Toronto.

Both my business partner and I had heard that there was a possibility that the building would never be built. This concerned us a great deal, as we were really looking forward to a completion of the project. I would have liked to have lived in the unit, and entertained the idea of buying out my partner's interest, if he was agreeable.

The delay in construction of the building had caused me extreme inconvenience and seriously jeopardized my investment, as I was unable to complete the deal, rent the unit, or purchase it for my own use. Due to delays in the start of construction, we listed our interest in the unit for sale on March 8, 1988, for $349,500. The real estate broker was Johnston & Daniel Limited, with the sales representative being Jurij Senyshyn. We had every intention to inform the developer once we had a bona fide buyer. The real estate agent reassured us that a listing of our interest was not in contravention of the terms of our agreement.

In a relatively brief time period, the developer became aware of our listing, and informed us that the listing contravened the terms of the agreement of purchase and sale. The agreement was terminated with our deposits as liquidated damages, in spite of our attempts to clarify our position that we had not assigned our interest in the development, and that a listing did not constitute a sale.

I had not experienced this predicament before. The only lawyer I knew handled primarily real estate closings, and he suggested registering a caution on this property. We had one other option – walk away from our deposit of over $20,000 which was a fair amount of money in 1988.

In May 1988, after much deliberation, I decided to follow my lawyer's recommendation, and registered a caution on the developer's property at 400 Bloor Street East. The caution was to prevent the developer from dealing with the proposed condominium property by way of sale, mortgage, or otherwise. The lawyer claimed that this was necessary to protect our rights under our Agreement of Purchase & Sale that we had entered into with the developer. In hindsight, and based on the advice of a new lawyer, I believe it would have been more appropriate for us to have registered a certificate of pending litigation instead of a caution.

The purchaser of Suite 1602, in *BloorEast*, registered a certificate of pending litigation on August 25, 1988, against the developer for specific performance of their agreement of purchase and sale, or, in the alternative, damages for breach of contract in the amount of $200,000 reimbursement of moneys paid by the purchaser, a declaration that the purchaser hold an equitable lien in the lands, pre and post judgement interest, and their costs of legal action.

Based on my discussion with one of the purchasers, a group of seventeen purchasers in this project had retained a Toronto lawyer, David Roebuck, of Roebuck Garbig, for a class action lawsuit against the developer, and added Martin Atkins' name to that suit. The group's lawyer indicated that the group did not wish to have our claim added to theirs, as it would delay their action against the developer.

Other purchasers perhaps settled with the developer and may have been satisfied to get their deposits returned. Mr. Roebuck's office indicated that he could not add my name to the class action suit, as the class action was somewhat different from my legal claim.

It was clear to me that Guided Investments Limited had breached the trust that we and other purchasers had placed in them. They had failed to act responsibly in matters related to the *BloorEast* project, and concealed material facts, as well as misled us and other purchasers as to the actual progress of the project.

The developer had retained Mr. David Rubin, of Pallett Valo, Barristers & Solicitors, from their office in Mississauga, Ontario. The lawyer was not conciliatory based on his response to our claim and as evidenced by the developer's counterclaim. According to my discussions with a purchaser in *BloorEast*, that developer's lawyer was a "bully."

On June 6, 1989, the developer's lawyer filed a Notice of Appeal to delete the caution that was placed by me against title to the developer's lands. Subsequent to a hearing, the caution was allowed to stay on title.

After making a call to a large, well-known downtown Toronto legal firm, I was able to retain a new lawyer. In June 1989, my lawyer, Iler, Campbell & Associates, filed a Statement of Claim against the developer, Guided Investments Limited. I heard that the developer was having financial problems and the company could be headed for bankruptcy. My legal fees, including land transfer tax to register a caution, was about $10,500.

Mel H. Castelin

During 1988-89, I had sent a series of letters to various individuals in government and elsewhere to identify the issues, and seek their assistance, for a resolution of this matter.

They included Ms. Nadine Nowlan, City of Toronto Councillor for Ward 13, who contacted the city solicitor, Mr. Dennis Perlin, and the Minister of Consumer and Commercial Relations, Mr. William Wrye. Mr Wrye had responded to Ms. Nowlan on January 10, 1989, indicating that his office staff had received a reply from Howard Dixon of Guided Investments, who stated that the delay of the *BloorEast* project was because of a technical design problem with the foundation due to the proximity of the adjoining property building, and that the design problem was expected to be resolved by the middle of February 1989 (eight and a half months after the date of proposed construction of the building) at which time construction of the building was to go for tendering. The City of Toronto's Department of Buildings and Inspections had indicated that the development and collateral agreements for the *BloorEast* project were registered in the registry office on November 3, 1987, and the developer had applied for a building permit on May 9, 1988; however, as of November 2, 1988, a building permit was not issued. The City indicated that the development and collateral agreements did not give it the authority to require the developer to commence and carry out construction of *BloorEast*. As the project was within a site plan control area, the City's approval was required of certain categories of plans or drawings, and the developer was required to fulfill the obligations therein only if it constructed the building.

The City Solicitor had indicated that the City had recommended to the Provincial Government for legislative amendments giving greater consumer protection to condominium unit purchasers, and that was being considered by the Ministry of Consumer and Commercial Relations.

As I was extremely upset with the position taken by the developer, I contacted the following: the Federal Government's Minister of Justice, Mr. Doug Lewis; the Minister of Consumer and Commercial Relations, Mr. William Wrye; the Minister of the Attorney General, Mr. Ian Scott; Better Business Bureau; Urban Development Institute; Toronto Home Builders Association; Ontario Home Builders Association; The Globe and Mail; The Toronto Star; and The Toronto Sun. The consensus was that this matter was best dealt with through legal means.

The Ministry of Consumer and Commercial Relations indicated that the condominium matter, brought to their attention by me, highlighted the imbalance between the development industry and purchasers. In view of the imbalance, the Ministry of Consumer and Commercial Relations was considering a review of the Condominium Act.

On September 26, 1989, my lawyer sent a letter to the developer's lawyer informing him that the delivery time for the developer's statement of defence had expired, and he had until September 29, 1989, failing which it would be legally noted as being in default. My lawyer received a reply the next day in the form of the developer's statement of defence.

On September 5, 1990, we retained another lawyer, David Payne, of *Adler, Payne*, in Toronto. Mr. Payne was already representing another purchaser in *BloorEast*, and we felt retaining him could be a consolidated action, and of benefit to both parties.

The developer filed its statement of defence wherein it indicated we had breached the terms of our Agreement of Purchase and Sale by listing our interest for sale, and by registering a caution on the developer's lands. The developer made a counterclaim for $1 million. On May 28, 1991, Mr. David

Rubin sent our lawyer an Offer to Settle, which was open for acceptance until May 31, 1991. As per the instructions from his client, it represented one last offer to settle our claim before they commenced discoveries. Essentially, the offer was not acceptable to us and we refused to settle.

On June 4, 1991, Mr. Payne sent a letter to Mr. David Rubin, informing him that an examination for discovery of a representative of Guided Investments Limited was scheduled to take place on July 22, 1991, at the offices of Legal Transcript Services Ltd., at 120 Adelaide Street West, Toronto. I was informed that the discovery went ahead as scheduled. The next day, we received a new Offer to Settle.

On July 23, 1991, Mr. Davis Rubin sent our lawyer a new Offer to Settle which was open for acceptance until July 26, 1991, and was to be accepted at the same time by us and the other plaintiff in this matter.

It was quite obvious to us that the developer had offered the other plaintiff a better deal and driven a wedge between the other plaintiff and us, as they had asked that the offers be accepted by both plaintiffs. As the other plaintiff wanted to settle, it left us in a very precarious position.

On October 2, 1991, Mr. Payne informed me that our legal matter was scheduled for hearing on October 10, 1991. On October 23, 1991, we agreed to a settlement and Mutual Release. The terms of the release prohibited us from disclosing the amount of the settlement to anyone other than Revenue Canada.

Summary

Buying a condominium apartment in Toronto seemed like a simple matter. However, sometimes there can be a serious turn of events that can radically alter the entire process.

This chapter provides a brief example of how the "big players" operate, and how easy it is for a "little person" to get eliminated in the real estate business in Toronto.

In the 1970s and 1980s, in the absence of well-planned rules, the development industry was like a sports team with few rules or referees, and no penalty boxes. Unchecked, the development industry was beginning to destroy their system, mopping up all the opportunities and pushing political leaders towards socialist alternatives. Unbridled, free enterprise devours some as surely as an un-officiated hockey game sidelines the most talented players in the game.

In the 1970s and 1980s there was an imbalance between the development industry and purchasers. In response to complaints from the public over the years, the provincial government tightened the rules, as evidenced by changes to the Condominium Act by the Ministry of Consumer and Commercial Relations.

By 1988, another event began to brew, and I will explain below.

Buying a condo based on an ad placed in the *Toronto Star,* dated March 5, 1988, by Ken and Vilma Curran

Ken and Vilma Curran had placed an ad for the assignment of their interest in a preconstruction condominium unit near the Don Valley Parkway in Toronto (North York). Ken Curran was the

Mel H. Castelin

Superintendent of Employee Relations of the Metropolitan Toronto School Board. I attempted to obtain details of that condo, including the price. The condo was to be my principal residence. I had made my phone calls in April 1988 from London, Ontario, where I was working during the weekdays on a project.

In April 1988, my friend, Bill Proskos, and I met with William Bray of a Toronto law firm to let him know we were going to retain him for our real estate matters. He agreed to it.

My phone calls, in response to that ad, resulted in my arranging an initial meeting with Mr. Curran at the condominium developer's sales office in North York, in order to view the project and make sure the development was a bona fide one. I obtained some basic information such as a floor plan and project brochure, and informed him that I would look at them. Thereafter, I attempted to obtain further information but was told by Mrs. Curran that her husband was in negotiations on a Toronto School Board matter at a downtown Toronto hotel. After several attempts, I was successful in meeting Mr. Curran at the Four Seasons Hotel, in Yorkville, on May 1, 1988. I obtained a copy of the assignment agreement and placed a call from Mr. Curran's room to William Bray, to arrange a meeting. He agreed to meet on May 1, 1988, to review the assignment agreement. William Bray reviewed the document on May 1st and said it was clean. I had asked him what I should do next, and he asked me to convey a signed agreement and a cheque for $10,000 to the Currans, which I personally delivered to Mrs. Curran that day.

Essentially, Ken and Vilma Curran had committed a fraud by attempting to convey their worthless interest in a condo unit for $62,491, and knowingly concealing material facts as they failed to attach important schedules to the Agreement of Purchase and Sale. Furthermore, Ken Curran had claimed that the schedules were unimportant extensions of the closing date. In fact, they were not mere extensions to the closing date but gave the developer the right to extend the closing date in order to obtain rezoning for the condominium development, and increase the price of the unit. In other words, the schedules gave the developer the right to end the agreement of purchase and sale with the Currans, which would have made their assignment worthless. This information was known by Mr. Curran, as there had previously been a potential buyer who had obtained the information about those schedules through their lawyer, with Mr. Curran's lawyer being fully aware of them. That buyer decided not to proceed, upon knowing the details of the schedules.

My lawyer, Mr. Paul Henry, stated in his letter to the Currans' lawyer that she should seriously consider withdrawing as counsel for the Currans, as the same law firm's lawyer, Mr. K. Ivan, was going to be a witness at the upcoming trial, and he held in his files documents that were important and germane to this case, namely of benefit to me.

But Mr. Curran and his new lawyer, Connie Fellow in Toronto, chose to conceal that information, and, in essence, perjured themselves. Slowly, the facts began to surface to my benefit, as my lawyer and I began to unraveled information which proved to be critical in this case.

The Currans never returned an executed copy of the Assignment Agreement. Curran and his wife lied about certain information during the discoveries in order to strengthen their case. In essence, both the lawyers for the defendants Curran and William Bray, had established a tag team as defendants, hoping they could pull it off with the clout of an established lawyer appointed by the law society.

Consequently, I initiated a legal claim against the Currans, and my lawyer William Bray, for negligence. William Bray was subsequently represented by Nicky Plank, a lawyer appointed by the Law Society of Upper Canada to represent him. I went through several lawyers before I found a reliable and competent one, namely Paul Henry of Chappell, Bushell, Stewart. In March 1994, Mr. Henry indicated that he was going to call as witness representatives of Concord Square who would say that Mr. and Mrs. Curran were advised in detail the reasons for the two amendments to their Agreement of Purchase and Sale. Also to be called as a witness, was Mr. W. B. Ivan, the Curran's lawyer at the time. It was clear that the Currans were aware that the developer's property had to be rezoned by June 30, 1988, or the Agreement of Purchase and Sale was at an end. It was clear that Mr. Curran did not bring the amendments to his agreement for the meeting with me because he did not want me to review them.

The most painful process of the lawsuit was going through the discoveries; I was cross examined by the defendant William Bray's lawyer on insignificant or miniscule details which had the effect of making the discovery proceedings very lengthy. Also, I was very upset since I knew that Mr. Curran had intentionally lied in his discovery hearing about critical information so that he would not have to return the funds I had paid him, or pay for damages. The intent of the lawyer for defendant William Bray was to absolve him of negligence. William Bray concealed the fact that he was to represent me, from the time he had reviewed the assignment agreement on May 1, 1988, through to final closing of the transaction. Instead, he arbitrarily chose to be retained by me when he wanted to do so in order to avoid a claim for negligence.

My investigation of certain events involved contacting the Four Seasons Hotel in Yorkville to obtain telephone records to show evidence of a phone call being made to William Bray's office from Mr. Curran's room. The telephone records were critical, as they were evidence I had met with Mr. Curran, and that I had made a call to William Bray on May 1, 1988, and the content of that call, if necessary. However, much to my disappointment, I was told that there had been a fire at the Four Seasons Hotel, and the records were not available.

In addition, Mr. Paul Henry and I decided to call several witnesses, and had the Ontario Court/Sheriff's Office serve our witnesses a notice to appear at the upcoming trial in 1994. In my mind and heart, I knew the defendants had lied about critical issues. So, the only avenue for me was to call witnesses who would have corroborated my claim, the effect of which would have been detrimental to the Currans.

The case was to go to trial after Easter Sunday in 1994, a time period of about six years from the filing of my Statement of Claim. The matter had gone to pre-trial, and in March 1994, my lawyer informed me that the lawyers for the defendants were prepared to make an offer. It was the day before Good Friday when my lawyer called me to his office to discuss the settlement offer he had received. If the offer was not accepted, the case was to go to trial the next week. Upon the advice of my lawyer, I decided to settle rather than go through a trial, as there would have been some risk in obtaining the full amount in my statement of claim.

Summary

Buying a preconstruction condominium apartment unit in Toronto can be a somewhat simple matter. However, events don't always turn out the way one anticipates. The system has changed from one that was designed to protect the development industry, to a more balanced one where purchasers are protected to a large degree. But one still has to be careful, as evidenced in this chapter which indicates how a highly esteemed person will distort facts, even when faced with the possibility of going to court.

By 2015, Premier Kathleen Wynne said that the Province of Ontario "will work with" the Law Society of Upper Canada to address questions about whether the professional regulator is adequately protecting the public from bad lawyers. In 2014, the Toronto Star investigation revealed that more than 230 lawyers were sanctioned by the law society over the past decade for criminal activity. The Toronto Star found that most were reprimanded, suspended, or disbarred, but fewer than one in five were charged criminally.

A forensic auditor with the Law Society, John Cottrell, told the *Toronto Star* that investigators were overwhelmed with too many cases, and were under pressure to meet monthly targets and close files quickly. (Source: *South Asian Focus,* October 9, 2014 – Law Society of Upper Canada caseload).

I did not need the next event to happen, after all of the other events in my life, while I was working in London, Ontario.

The tenant in a condo suite I owned at 360 Bloor Street East, Toronto, became a "tenant from hell"

A Toronto based company, operated by consultants Brenda and Eliza Bookbinder and Isabelle Harper, that specialized in the rental of downtown condos had found a tenant for a condo suite I owned at 360 Bloor Street East, Toronto. The tenant was Don Burns who did voice-overs and had worked for a country music radio station as an announcer. In less than ten months, he turned out to be a "tenant from hell."

The lease of my condo unit with Don Burns was for a term of one year. After about nine months, I did not receive the rental payments for the remainder of the first year, even though the tenant was still occupying my condo unit. It turned out that he reportedly had a form of throat cancer. On one occasion, when I went over to inspect the unit, I was met at the door by a woman in lingerie, which I assumed was his girlfriend; she claimed Don Burns was not there and I was unable to inspect my condo.

The worst part of this episode was when a friend of his had called him and he did not answer the phone, they contacted the building concierge. However, they could not open the suite door, as Don Burns had changed the door lock without giving a duplicate key to management. As Don Burns' car was still parked in the parking garage, his friend thought something had happened to him inside my condo. A call was made to the police, with the result being that the Toronto Fire Department came over and broke down the front door but found no one there. I found out later that Don Burns was away in New York.

The tenant, Don Burns, had made deals with people in the building so he could remain in my condo apartment. I was out of town and working in London, Ontario, and was unaware of the day-to-day tenant's episodes that were occurring. I was informed that the local hospital would return him to my condo, after he had been admitted to hospital regarding his emergency health issues.

The Landlord and Tenant Act provided for an eviction process and I had ample grounds to use the provision of the Act, which I did through my lawyer. I was eventually able to evict the tenant, after the due process of law took effect. It cost me legal fees, a loss of rental income for several months, and costs to fix the suite due to damages done by the tenant. There were burn marks in the carpet, and the mirror on the back of the door had been broken when the fire department broke open the front suite door, assuming that the tenant was inside the apartment. The apartment was a mess; a temporary suite door was installed until such time as the typical condominium suite door arrived. There was junk left behind by the tenant, namely some girly magazines. While I was in the apartment, a resident came over to claim some furniture he had loaned the tenant. I later learned that this tenant had made deals with a number of people in the building by selling his possessions, including a Rolex watch and other items in order to pay for his daily living expenses.

Summary

Renting a condo unit in Toronto may seem like an easy task. However, one has to screen prospective tenants in order to find a reliable one. Even if one is able to find a proper tenant, there is no guaranty that a tenant will make all of the rent payments during the tenure of the lease, or that a tenant will keep the unit in good condition, other than normal wear and tear.

The law in Ontario is stacked in favour of tenants, and against landlords. Most tenants are aware of this factor and some take full advantage of the situation.

Generally, property that is leased is not looked after in the same way as when it is owner-occupied. The terrible memories and turmoil I had experienced propelled me to sell my condo unit, which is what I eventually did. Fortunately, I was able to sell it for a modest gain.

If travel and Asia are of interest to you, you will read of my incredible experiences in the next chapter.

CHAPTER 6

An Incredible Journey to Goa

As I was in need of a vacation, and after being convinced to select Goa by my relatives, I made the necessary travel arrangements for our trip in October 1997. Goa is great for a vacation in October, since the bulk of tourists have not made their way to the coastal state, and hotels and many restaurants in the coastal areas are preparing for the eventual flow of tourists from Europe and elsewhere. Furthermore, the monsoon season comes to an end by late September. I was fortunate to be able to travel with my family due to the duration of the journey of over 30 hours of flying and layover time.

The ambiance of Goa thoroughly appealed to me. My stay there was made all the more enjoyable by the fact that the food did not disagree with me and I kept well, in spite of the presence of mosquitoes and other issues. But my vacation was short-lived, as I had to attend to various chores for my aunt Evelyn who was living in the ancestral house in Goa. This property was held under title of my great grandfather, and, over the years, was lived in by my great grandfather's children, my mother, and her sister, brother, and parents. It is a two storey Portuguese style house which was once one of the nicest houses in the neighbourhood. It was admired by the local residents and those that came to visit. But, in 1997, I was surprised, and deeply touched, to see the frail state of my aunt and the condition of the ancestral house which had not been maintained for a long time.

The roof was leaking and pests were present. Most of the fruit trees in the compound had stopped bearing fruit, and the house had lost most of its charm which existed in the 1960s and 1970s.

In order to settle a rather delicate ancestral property matter, I spoke with a lawyer who was recommended by a lawyer in Canada. Essentially, my aunt needed a suitable place in which to live where she would not be bothered by the in-laws. The matter was compounded by the fact that my aunt did not want to move from the ancestral house, as she and her parents had lived there most of her life. I hoped she would change her mind, but she did not, in spite of repeated attempts by me and many other people. In order to obtain appropriate legal advice, we decided to retain a lawyer so that an agreement could be reached for the ancestral property, and my aunt could live peacefully.

My aunt pleaded with me to help her and promised to convey her interest in the ancestral house to me. I undertook the matter as I saw her condition and did not want squatters to take over ownership of the property. My aunt had asked me if she should allow a local resident to occupy a portion of the property, which I advised against. My intention was to obtain consent from my in-laws to sell the property and use the proceeds to fund my aunt's living expenses, including her daily expenses, medical costs, and caretaker expenses, or costs for eventually living in a retirement home.

On the following pages are photographs of the Goa ancestral house and several scenic locations in Goa.

VIEW OF THE VERANDA AND ENTRANCE TO THE TWO STOREY
ANCESTRAL HOUSE IN GOA

A FRONT VIEW OF THE TWO STORY ANCESTRAL HOUSE,
IN GOA, IN 1997

MY AUNT EVELYN AT 87 YEARS NEXT TO HER RELIGIOUS
PHOTOS IN THE ANCESTRAL HOUSE

HOTEL GOAN HERITAGE, CALANGUTE, GOA

VIEW OF COLVA BEACH, SOUTH GOA

GOA SCIENCE CENTRE WITH A LUXURY CONDO BUILDING IN
THE BACKGROUND

A BEAUTIFUL PARK ACROSS THE ROAD FROM THE GOA
SCIENCE CENTRE

VIEW OF DONA PAULA, AN AFFLUENT RESIDENTIAL ENCLAVE
SOUTH OF PANAJI, GOA

A LUXURY HOTEL KNOWN AS AGUADA HERMITAGE – FORT
AGUADA BEACH RESORT, GOA

BOM JESUS BASILICA, OLD GOA

The Basilica of Bom Jesus is located in Old Goa and is a UNESCO World Heritage Site. The basilica holds the mortal remains of St. Francis Xavier. Old Goa was the capital of Goa in the early days of Portuguese rule. *Bom Jesus* (literally, 'Good or Holy Jesus') was the name used by the Portuguese when they were in Goa. The Jesuit church is India's first minor basilica, and is considered to be one of the best examples of baroque architecture in India. The church contains the body of St. Francis Xavier, a very close friend of St. Ignatius Loyola, with whom he founded the Society of Jesus (the Jesuits). Francis Xavier died on Sancian Island while en route to continental China on December 2, 1552. The body of Francis Xavier was first taken to Portuguese Malacca, and two years later shipped back to Goa. It is said that the saint's body was as fresh as the day it was buried. The remains of the saint still attract a huge number of devotees, Christian and non-Christian alike, from all over the world, especially during the public viewing of his body every ten years (last held in 2014). The saint is said to have miraculous powers of healing.

My travel to Goa in 1997 lead to a complicated turn of events

In October 1997, I was surprised to see the terrible state of my aunt Evelyn, the condition of the ancestral house, and a lack of funds for my aunt's survival, which had dwindled since the demise of her parents who died in 1961 and 1984, and her brother Isaac who passed away in 1987. To prevent my aunt from being defrauded by people in Goa, and because no one showed interest in looking after my aunt Evelyn, I retained a lawyer by the name of Advocate Edwin Furtado, in 1997, to resolve the ancestral property matter based on the recommendation of my lawyer in Toronto.

However, after one year, he had barely worked on this matter. Therefore, on my second trip to Goa in 1999, I retained a second lawyer by the name of Advocate Benny Nazareth, on the recommendation of a Goa priest, Father Manuel Pinto Do Rosario. I instructed him by email to resolve the title matter in order to settle the ancestral property matter. My intention was to use the proceeds of the sale of the ancestral house to pay my in-laws in Canada their share, and for my aunt Evelyn's living expenses and care, as well as to defray some of my expenses for attending to this matter.

In mid-1995, my aunt Evelyn had been defrauded of about $8,000 from her bank accounts by her helper and social worker in Goa, Gurudas Satoskar. The equivalent in Indian currency is about Rs 2 lakh, which is a huge amount in Goa. On one of my mother's trips to Goa, she saw a resident that lives there try to remove the house property limit, or what we refer to in survey terms as a standard iron bar, in an attempt to alter the legal boundary of the ancestral property.

In spite of my family's repeated pleas, my aunt Evelyn did not want to move; so, I could not sell the property. My aunt Evelyn and my mother pleaded with me to assist them, so that my aunt could live a peaceful life for the few remaining years of her life. Therefore, in September and November 2000, when I spoke to my in-law in Canada, she was in agreement to selling the ancestral property, and she had indicated that she would wait to see how much money was being placed in her sons' names from the said sale.

A relative indicated her interest in looking after my aunt Evelyn in lieu of the transfer of the house to them, but my aunt Evelyn did not want children living in the house with her. This relative indicated that she had received a letter from my in-law in Canada, who had indicated her refusal to sell the house to them.

In 1999, I approached the local priest (Father Manuel Pinto Do Rosario), hoping he, or any other priest, would look after my aunt Evelyn in lieu of the house being conveyed to them, but we were unable to secure an agreement with them. Thereafter, I approached the local nuns and spoke with a Sister A. Lawrence, in Goa, to see if they would look after my aunt Evelyn. I never heard back from them, and when I called the nuns, they indicated they were not interested.

As a final attempt, I spoke to a local charitable group through Mr. Savio Mascarenhas, a manager of the former ICDS Bank in Goa. That charitable group had shown interest in looking after my aunt in lieu of the property being conveyed to them. When they eventually got back to me, they indicated the property was not suitable to them.

Essentially, the local priests, nuns, and a charitable group, showed no interest in looking after my aunt Evelyn. In addition, I could not renovate the ancestral house, as I did not have clear title to it, and the costs of renovation were considerable. Even a developer in Goa did not want to redevelop the ancestral property in the absence of clear title, due to the risk of construction being halted in midstream. My aunt Evelyn had to undergo a considerable amount of hardship due to the atrocious condition of the ancestral house, and her deteriorating health.

Attending to this matter had cost me a very significant sum of money and time off work without pay, as I had to take many flights to Goa to attend to the legal issues, make sure my aunt Evelyn was being looked after and not taken advantage of by some people, and to arrange some house repairs. But the significantly long period of time the legal matter took, namely 17 years, was what was so emotionally draining and financially costly for me.

Incidentally, my mother's brother, Isaac, had sold most of the ancestral properties in Goa before his mother's death, and eventually his death, to provide funds for his mother and sister Evelyn. The absence of proper estate planning resulted in a lack of funds to support his mother and sister. This was compounded by a high rate of inflation in Goa, which resulted in ones savings being depleted quickly. The ancestral house would have been the only source of funds for the continued care of my uncle's mother Caroline, and his sister Evelyn. Unfortunately, my uncle Isaac's demise in 1987 prevented a solution and closure of this long-standing matter. The unresolved matter caused me extreme hardship, significant financial costs, and serious health problems.

By late 2013, I received a significant blow due to the following reasons: The lawyer attending to the legal proceeding in Goa had messed up the legal proceedings of the ancestral property; I encountered a loss in my business income; inability to focus on my job; a tremendous level of stress; loss of sleep due to the need for numerous phone calls to Goa between midnight and 2 a.m.; time off work to travel to Goa; and a lack of closure to this long-standing matter. I had to take anti-nausea tablets (Gravol) to fly to Goa. However, the side effects of Gravol are unpleasant, especially due to the lengthy duration and multiple flights to Goa. Long distance flying is not something I would want to undertake again.

My aunt Evelyn was incapable of handling property or financial matters. These matters should have been properly attended to by the appropriate persons to prevent the source of the terrible financial and health problems of my grandmother Caroline and aunt Evelyn. My uncle Isaac was only four years old when my granduncle died, and 29 years when his father died. The main issue is that there was no legal will for the entire ancestral property, and the in-laws assumed that the entire ancestral property was their sole inheritance.

Based on the flawed legal proceeding and position taken by the advocate, I spoke to the Deputy Chief Minister of Goa at the Goa Legislature Secretariat in July 2015, and, in August 2015, informed him of the extraordinary length of time it took for the legal proceeding, and possible fraud by the advocate with respect to the funds I had sent him, which represented the other party's share under the Inventory Proceeding.

My new lawyer advised me that the Chief Minister would not likely be able to do much, so the best option would be to initiate criminal proceedings against the advocate. However, my personal presence in Goa would have been necessary for that process. My sources also indicated that filing a complaint with the Goa police in my absence would not be productive because the Goa police would not take any action in my absence, and there is no guarantee the Goa police would pursue the matter, even if I was present in Goa.

Corruption in Goa

Foreigners Infiltrate Goa

The blatant misuse of the Foreign Direct Investment (FDI) route by Russian nationals to grab prime land in Goa had become a cause of concern and even a security threat. A FDI is a controlling ownership in a business enterprise in one country by an entity based in another country. The situation is compounded by the fact that certain politicians like former Goa Minister, Babush Monserrate, allegedly legalized land conversions for a price and let fraudulent companies operate unchecked.

International mafia and terror groups were investing in Indian real estate, according to the National Security Advisor (NSA). A report by the NSA stated that the Russian mafia had invested large sums of money in Goa real estate, and the FDI was getting automatic approval. Individuals, such as Leonid Beyzer, Yulia Yaskova, Sergey Ivanov, Valiulin Rashid, and Mamedov, are familiar names of the Russian mafia operating in the Goa real estate industry. They have connections with local lawyers who can solve the problems, as foreigners are not allowed to do real estate business in India. These lawyers help the Russian mafia break Indian laws and breach national security.

One way business is being conducted is by forming a company and having the company buy property. In another instance, dummy Indian partners are used to buy land such as True Axiz and Artlibori Resorts. Wrong local and foreign addresses were used in the documents, and the records of foreign investment were not properly maintained. This is done to hide criminal records. Leonid Beyzer was charged in Russia for possession of hashish and Sergey Ivanov set up a bank called OTON that defrauded hundreds of investors.(Source: *CNN-IBN*, June 16, 2007)

Politicians and Kickbacks

Investigations into tax evasion by a former government official have unraveled that a minister in the Cabinet of former Goa Chief Minister, Digambar Kamat, received huge payoffs from a complex nexus of land sharks, who set up a web of fictitious transactions to give their kickbacks. According to an Income Tax assessment order and notice served on former Goa civil service official, N. Suryanarayana, in December 2011, by Income Tax Deputy Commissioner, V S Chakrapani, Babush Monserrate received over Rs 26.58 crore (about $6 million) in cash and kind, to convert huge tracts of orchard and agricultural lands into settlement zones in early 2006, when he was Town and Country Planning Minister in the BJP government. A document seized by Income Tax officials from N. Suryanarayana's residence in Caranzalem reveals it all. It says that in January 2006, N. Suryanarayana, and friends, formed a *syndicate* to deal in properties within and outside Goa. It leaves little room for doubt about how Goa is being quartered and sold to real estate syndicates from outside the state by local land sharks. N. Suryanarayana was asked to pay a tax of Rs 10 crore (about $2.2 million).

After picking up 60 acres of orchard land in Old Goa in March 2006, through Pradeep Palekar, Managing Director of Primeslots Properties, N. Suryanarayana, and company, approached Sadiq Shaik of Essar Builders, known for his direct links with Monserrate. N. Suryanarayana, who was known to be close to Monserrate while he served in the government till 2005, when he resigned for the more lucrative business of real estate brokering, indicated that an amount of Rs 24.75 crore (about $5.5 million) was paid to convert 11 huge properties across Goa (they were spread across Old Goa, Verna, Siridao, Porvorim, Galgibag, Quelossim, Cavelossim, Varca, Majorda, Dona Paula and Pilerne). "Out of the above amount of Rs 24.75 crore, an amount of Rs 19.75 crore was paid during the period of April 2006 to August 2006 to Sadiq Shaik at his residence in Dona Paula and in the office of Dinar Tarcar (chairman of Landscape Group) at Campal, Panaji," the seized document says. The Income Tax order tracks the money trail to Monserrate, made through a convoluted process by Shaik, who set up a fictitious company using his restaurateur brother, Shiraz Shaik, and a friend. Sadiq Shaik conveyed Rs 26,58,16,250 (about $6 million) "in kind and in cash to Atanasio (Babush) Monserrate indirectly," according to the order. Shaik transferred land at Sancoale worth Rs 11.58 crore (about $2.6 million) to Monserrate's son's company Good Earth Developers, and provided an advance of Rs 15 crore (about $3.3 million) to Raj Hospitality Pvt. Ltd., in which Monserrate, his wife Jennifer, and son, are directors. Monserrate, who was forced to resign from the ministry in January 2007, following huge protests against the Regional Plan 2011, did not deliver on the land conversion promises, and N. Suryanarayana and his syndicate are still trying to recover the money through Sadiq Shaikh. N. Suryanarayana's lawyers have in fact gone to court to recover the Rs 4.99 crore (about $1.1 million) paid by cheque. In April 2009, Monserrate was detained by the Mumbai Customs for trying to take a huge amount of foreign currency out of the country. Both he and his wife Jennifer were front-runners for Congress tickets for the March 3, 2012 election. Dinar Tarcar, who has also been in the news for illegal mining, has his name linked to the BJP in this election. N. Suryanarayana, who had a controversial track record in the Goa government, has been asked to pay Rs 10.57 crore (about $2.3 million) in tax for the years 2007-2008. A hearing on the matter scheduled for January 17, 2012, did not take place. (Source: Devika Sequeira, *Deccan* Herald, January 30, 2010)

UK parliament debates massive corruption in Goa

The *Hindustan Times*, dated January 29, 2015, reported that a debate in the Westminster Hall of the House of Commons, in London, on January 27, 2015, highlighted the problems faced by hundreds of British citizens who had acquired property in Goa, and had started businesses, but were now at the centre of demands for bribery and inquiries. Terming the situation as the *Goan equivalent of the mafia*, British Conservative Member of Parliament, Tim Loughton, indicated that British citizens had met all requirements before acquiring property and starting businesses in Goa, but were told by officials that the properties had been acquired illegally. Loughton stated: "The problem seems to be quite widespread, with a number of British expats suffering such consequences. It has been suggested that there are in excess of 300 similar cases that we know about. Huge stress is being caused to people who legitimately went out to invest in businesses in Goa." "The situation is proving to be a nice little earner for the government in Goa, and various government officials are pretty brazen in demanding money to make the problem, which is of their making, supposedly go away." Loughton reportedly named two officials of the Goa unit of the Enforcement Directorate in the context of corruption, and said he had repeatedly raised the matter with the Indian High Commission, Goa Chief Minister and Union Finance Minister, Arun Jaitley. Responding to the debate, Foreign Office Minister, Tobias Ellwood, recalled that until 2007, rules governing purchases of property by foreigners in Goa were open to misinterpretation. (Source: Prasun Sonwalkar, *Hindustan Times*, London)

Summary

Goa has wonderful people and a fabulous culture, and I met a few honourable people there. Today, unfortunately, Goa is among the most corrupt states in India. It was all started by the politicians and some senior Goa government officials. Not all the politicians and government workers are corrupt in Goa, but a big chunk of them is. Quite a big chunk of Goa government employees are also the relatives of the politicians or the senior officials. (Source: *The Times of India*, November 27, 2014)

From the foregoing, it is evident that having a proper will and power of attorney are paramount for families. A will should be updated and the current intention of the grantor should be reflected.

The property boom in Goa has been attracting a lot of investors, and with gorgeous sea facing apartments and villas, wonderful people, a mix of village life and a tourist hot spot, more and more people have been moving to Goa from within India and overseas. However, unscrupulous developments have also crept in. People buying have to ensure that they buy only quality construction with a clear title. It is critical that one hire a reputable local lawyer, as many older legal documents in Goa are in Portuguese, thanks to its colonial past.

Buying property in Goa is pretty straightforward if one or one's family is:

• An Indian, a Person of Indian Origin (PIO) or a Non-Resident Indian (NRI)

If one is not any of the above, one can still buy property if one's:

• company is registered and doing business in India
• company has an Indian office

If you intend to purchase property, the visa you enter India on is important as the type of visa should clearly indicate the intention to stay in India for an uncertain period to determine residential status. Do not buy property if you are on a tourist visa, and do not transfer funds illegally to buy property in Goa. Furthermore, there are restrictions on purchasing agricultural land, farmhouses and plantations. A foreigner who has purchased property in India without meeting all of the Government of India requirements, irrespective of whether the purchase was made in good faith, could face an investigation into the purchase and legal ownership of the property, which could in extreme circumstances lead to the property being

confiscated and returned to the Government of India and a
monetary penalty imposed.

If you believe that you have been subject to a property crime,
you should make a statement to the local police and obtain a
copy of the statement with the incident number. Please note,
there may be a time restriction between the time of the alleged
crime and the time within which you make your complaint.

One more issue about property in Goa. A translation of the
word "Pensão" in English means a kind of alimony or more
accurately a perennial alimony. Well, the situation is that many
properties and pieces thereof, held originally by Goans, prior to
an arrival of the Portuguese in Goa, were either donated to the
temple or church or relatives with a guarantee that the original
owner or donor (in more refined English, the "settlor") will
perennially receive some spiritual relief. The speculated relief
was in terms of donations to the temple or church most of the
time in the name of the settlor. In all the years of my existence
and travels to Goa, I did not bother to research and understand
the implications and the theology of this situation. The matter is
seriously looked upon by some people in Goa who are
fanatically religious or harbor jealousy and believe if one does
not contribute pensao, one was destined for some sort of curse,
ill-luck or ill-health. The fact is a "curse", if any, is a result of
people who harm one another by way of idle gossip, libel and
slander, harbouring a vendetta or legal proceedings including
those involving property disputes.

The ordeals I encountered in the workplace and in dealings
with financial advisors and others are described in the previous
chapters of this book. Fortunately, the events I experienced did
not turn me into an alcoholic or a consumer of street drugs. I
was able to withstand the pressure of being a plaintiff in several
court cases in Ontario and continue to work full-time as a real

estate appraiser. Perhaps the treatment I had encountered working in the government and in personal business dealings prepared me to deal with life's challenges because no program in school prepared me for them. However, while I contemplated the events I experienced over the years, I began to read a number of books which gave me a much better perspective. The next two chapters provide insight into a number of important issues.

Sources: *IBNLive*, Rohit Khanna & Pramod Acharya
Hindustan Times, January 29, 2015
Suraj Nandrekar & Basuri Desai, *Herald*, September 15, 2015

CHAPTER 7

Players, Politicians and Psychopaths

Financial Advisors

Large sums of money were lost by me when I retained financial advisors to manage my investments. One financial advisor included Richard Charlton of Fortune Financial Corporation in Oakville, who recommended I transfer my funds from one financial advisor in the same company, namely Fortune Financial Corporation, to him. His recommendation amounted to the "churning" of my funds. In addition, he recommended I borrow money to purchase mutual funds, which is another awful strategy.

Other investment advisors I dealt with were: Sam Panzures of The Financial Planning Group; David Chau of Golden Gate Funds; Ashish Gandhi of Investment Planning Council of Canada; Everest D'Sousa of Keybase Financial Group Inc.; Avin Mehra of CIBC Wood Gundy; and Elias Viola and Luis Flores of RBC Financial Group. Except for my account with Sam Panzures, the remaining investment strategies turned out to be net financial losses.

In 2005, I invested $10,000 in Golden Gate Funds. Ads claimed Golden Gate Funds were an investment in mortgages, promising 8% annual returns with almost no risk to the principal. In a series of letters, the OSC demanded Golden Gate comply with securities law by registering with the OSC, filing a proper prospectus, and begin reporting its operations; but that never happened. Due to the OSC's privacy rules, investors were never warned of Golden Gate's status. The Ontario Securities Commission, the agency that monitors and enforces investment laws, first opened an investigation when Golden Gate began marketing its funds to the public, as far back as 2005. In January 2009, after the collapse of Golden Gate, about four years after its investigation began, the Ontario Securities Commission launched formal hearings against Ernest Anderson and Golden Gate.

An investigation by the TV show W5, into Golden Gate Funds, uncovered a trail of broken lives and broken promises. The more than 150 investors lost more than $8 million when the mortgage investment company collapsed in 2007. The financial meltdown sparked investment industry investigations, accusations of deception, and ongoing questions about securities regulation and oversight. Many had invested more than $50,000; some had invested over $100,000, and one couple had invested $1,220,000, according to material obtained by me.

Golden Gate Funds was founded by Ernest Anderson, an Egyptian-born businessman with a flair for raising funds and flattering political friends. He claims a PhD in economics from Columbia University, a degree which *W5* was unable to verify. Living in a $4-million, 7,000 square foot mansion, north of Toronto, Anderson denied any wrongdoing and blamed the meltdown on market circumstances and on others who worked at Golden Gate.

But Milton Chambers, a lawyer Ernest Anderson hired as Golden Gate's in-house counsel, says this wasn't a case of gullible seniors making ill-informed investment decisions.

According to Chambers, "They were taken in the same way I was taken in." Chambers joined Golden Gate from 2003 to 2006, after Anderson invited him to a high-profile party for Paul Martin, Prime Minister of Canada. Anderson and his wife made large political donations to the Liberal Party – at least $10,000 in 2005 alone. He courted Conservatives as well, attending fundraisers and hiring high profile members of both parties. Milton Chambers believed that those kinds of connections impressed investors and lent sparkle to Golden Gate, as the investment fund attracted investors.

In 2007, the company took out an ad in the Globe and Mail, announcing a new high-profile Board of Directors, including former Prime Minister John Turner, former RCMP Commissioner Norman Inkster, and former Conservative Cabinet Minister John Reynolds. When *W5* contacted all three to confirm that they were directors of Golden Gate, they denied that they had ever agreed to sit on the company's board.

A Commission investigator told the hearing it "looks as though a certain amount of funds were spent on Mr. Anderson's lifestyle, for his personal expenses…it's our understanding Mr. Anderson did lease a Porsche, a limousine and a Bentley." In a joint Settlement Agreement signed with the Ontario Securities Commission in September 2009, Ernest Anderson admitted that there were no investments in mortgages. "Contrary to the Golden Gate Limited Partnership agreement, investor funds were not used to purchase an investment portfolio of mortgages. Investor money was transferred to the bank accounts of other related companies, and was used to pay operating costs for Golden Gate Funds LP and other related companies, as well as monthly interest payments to other investors, and to re-pay investors from a previous investment scheme operated by Anderson." Golden Gate's former in-house counsel, Milton Chambers, told *W5*, "It appears as if all of the money was used in the classic Ponzi scheme – in which new investors were paying out old investors. Or it was used to pay the ongoing expenses of the company for a period of three years."

The OSC ordered Ernest Anderson and Golden Gate Fund to pay nearly $4.8 million in fines and fees. There is no indication if any of the investors have been repaid. In an e-mail to W5, Ernest Anderson wrote, "What went wrong, market conditions, miss organization (sic) at the time I left the company to be run by others while I had to deal to some personal issues." *W5*'s investigation also uncovered some troubling information about Mr. Anderson's past. In 2005, he was convicted of sexual assault relating to an incident which took place at Golden Gates' offices. He also has civil court cases and judgments totalling more than $250,000 against him. (Source: Tom Popyk, *W5 – CTV News,* published April 24, 2010)

As a last resort, I invested my remaining savings with Don Yu, Financial Advisor & Insurance Co. He proved to be just as terrible an advisor as the previous ones and disputed with me about his investment approach, which proved to be a loss.

Therefore, I filed a complaint with the Ontario Securities Commission (OSC) against Don Yu Financial to settle this matter. The OSC heard my case, and after I appeared at a hearing before the OSC board members, the OSC issued sanctions and censure against Don Yu. Unfortunately, the OSC does not have the power to have an advisor reimburse an investor for financial losses due to receiving bad advice or negligence on the part of an advisor. That issue is left for the investor to settle through the courts.

The one person I would have trusted in this industry was Gerry Kowalchuk, who had left the real estate appraisal business to become a financial advisor with Merrill Lynch. I had known him when he was a practicing real estate appraiser with his firm, Doggett & Kowalchuk, in Thunder Bay, Ontario. Gerry Kowalchuk is no longer with Merrill Lynch but is listed as being a Vice-President, Investment Advisor with Wood Gundy. I happened to find him on YouTube where he posted a song called "Down By The Henry Moore."

David X. Li's Formula and Its Impact on Financial Markets

A Chinese mathematician, Dr. David X. Li, came up with a formula that seemed a godsend to Wall Street and the City of London financial manipulators. The formula, known to most economists and mathematical analysts with major banking houses, is unfamiliar to most, but like Einstein's formula, E=MC2 it is destined to become famous in history for the influence it had on human actions and policies. Known as a Gaussian copula function, Li's formula allowed hugely complex risks to be modeled with more ease and accuracy than ever before. Li made it possible for traders to sell vast quantities of new securities, expanding financial markets to unimaginable levels. His formula was adopted by a wide range of the financial market, from bond investors and Wall Street banks, to rating agencies and regulators. It became deeply entrenched in the system, and made people so much money that warnings about its limitations were largely ignored.

The model eventually fell apart when cracks started appearing early on, when financial markets began behaving in ways that users of Li's formula had not expected. The cracks became canyons in 2008, when ruptures in the financial system's foundations swallowed up trillions of dollars and put the survival of the global banking system in serious peril. Li's formula has gone down in history as instrumental in causing the unfathomable losses that brought the world financial system to its knees. (Source: *Babylon's Banksters* by Joseph P. Farrell – A Feral House book, 2010)

Wall Street and Washington

A prime example of how Wall Street and Washington are connected is evident in how senior officials slide between corporate and political positions. One example is Henry "Hank" Merritt Paulson, Jr., an American banker. He had served as the Chairman and Chief Executive Officer of Goldman Sachs. Hank Paulson left the top job at Goldman Sachs to become Treasury Secretary in 2006. He ended up almost single-handedly running the country's economic policy for the last year of the Bush administration. The three main gripes against Hank Paulson were that he was late in battling the financial crisis, he let Lehman Brothers fail, and he pushed through Congress a big bailout bill which has been a wasteful mess.

In 2009, the Federal Reserve failed to protect America's money supply. No governmental audit has been allowed since its inception, even though many have called for one, including consumer advocate Ralph Nader since the 1970s. There were even demands for an abolishment of the Federal Reserve. However, in 2012, the first-ever Government Accountability Office (GAO) audit of the Federal Reserve was carried out due to the Ron Paul, Alan Grayson Amendment to the Dodd-Frank bill, which passed in 2011. Essentially, Rep. Ron Paul was successful in bringing about the House of Representatives to vote to widen the government's powers to audit the Federal Reserve's activities.

The Board of Governors, the 12 Federal Reserve Banks, and the Federal Reserve System, as a whole, are all subject to several levels of audit and review. The lack of transparency of the Federal Reserve was due to the secret mixture of big money and power of the banking elite and the Federal Reserve who wanted to retain their absolute control. According to Ralph Nader, the decisions and policies of the Federal Reserve "affect the level of inflation, unemployment, home buying, consumer credit, and other prices consumers and workers must bear. It also adds up to how few or how many financial corporations will dominate the economy."

Ben Bernanke, Alan Greenspan, and various other bankers vehemently opposed an audit of the Federal Reserve, and lied to Congress about the effects an audit would have on markets. Nevertheless, what was revealed in the first audit in the Federal Reserve's nearly 100 year history was startling:

Sixteen trillion dollars ($16,000,000,000,000) had been secretly given out to US banks and corporations, and foreign banks from France to Scotland.

The three largest bailouts were given to US banks Citigroup, Morgan Stanley, and Merrill Lynch. From the period between December 2007 and June 2010, the Federal Reserve had secretly bailed out many of the world's banks, corporations, and governments. The Federal Reserve likes to refer to these secret bailouts as an all-inclusive loan program, but virtually none of the money has been returned, and it was loaned out at 0% interest.

Why the Federal Reserve had never been public about this, or even informed the United States Congress about the $16 trillion dollar bailout is obvious – the American public would have been outraged to find out that the Federal Reserve had bailed out foreign banks while Americans were struggling to find jobs.

To place $16 trillion into perspective, remember that the GDP of the United States is only about $14.12 trillion. The entire national debt of the United States government, spanning its 200+ year history, is about $14.5 trillion. The budget that was debated so heavily in Congress and the Senate was $3.5 trillion.

(Source: Beforeitsnews.com – September 1, 2012)

Politicians

It is common knowledge that well-paid lobbyists are used by corporations to continually lobby governments to facilitate their agenda, which involves businesses or controversial projects that are sometimes detrimental to the public.

The 1996 United States campaign finance controversy was an alleged effort by the People's Republic of China to influence domestic American politics prior to, and during, the President Bill Clinton administration, and also involved the fund-raising practices of the administration itself. While questions regarding the U.S. Democratic Party's fund-raising activities first arose over a *Los Angeles Times* article published on September 21, 1996, China's alleged role in the affair first gained public attention when Bob Woodward and Brian Duffy of *The Washington Post* published a story stating that a United States Department of Justice investigation into the fund-raising activities had uncovered evidence that agents of China sought to direct contributions from foreign sources to the Democratic National Committee (DNC) before the 1996 presidential campaign. The journalists wrote that intelligence information had shown the Chinese embassy in Washington, D.C. was used for coordinating contributions to the DNC in violation of United States law forbidding non-American citizens or non-permanent residents from giving monetary donations to United States politicians and political parties.

Taiwan-born Maria Hsia, a California immigration consultant and a long time fund raiser for Al Gore, facilitated $100,000 in illegal campaign contributions through her efforts at Hsi Lai Temple, a Chinese Buddhist temple associated with Taiwan in Hacienda Heights, California. This money went to the DNC, to the Clinton-Gore campaign, and to Patrick Kennedy. After a trial, she was convicted in March 2000. The Democratic National Committee eventually returned the money donated by the Temple's monks and nuns. Twelve nuns and employees of the temple, including temple abbess Venerable Yi Kung (who resigned her post after being subpoenaed), refused to answer questions by pleading the Fifth Amendment when they were subpoenaed to testify before Congress.

Two other Buddhist nuns admitted destroying lists of donors and other documents related to the controversy because they felt the information would embarrass the Temple. A Temple-commissioned videotape of the fund raiser also went missing and the nuns' attorney claimed it may have been shipped off to Taiwan. (Source: Wikipedia)

In Ontario, there has been a lot of controversy about the Liberal government over the past few years. Laura Miller, former deputy chief of staff to then-premier Dalton McGuinty, is set to go to trial in September 2017, for her alleged role in the Ontario's gas plants scandal, but first she is going to help B.C. Premier Christy Clark win re-election in a vote expected in early May of 2017. David Livingston, former Premier Dalton McGuinty's chief of staff at the time, is also set to go to trial alongside Miller for their alleged role in the deletion of emails related to the cancellation of two gas plants in the Greater Toronto Area. They each face one count of breach of trust, one of mischief in relation to data, and one count of misuse of a computer system to commit the offence of mischief. Both have declared their innocence and have said they will fight the charges in court. (Source: Ashley Csanady, *National Post*, September 13, 2016)

Ontario's Liberal government faces a $1-billion lawsuit for imposing a moratorium on offshore wind farms, as SouthPoint Wind filed suit in Ontario Superior Court of Justice in Windsor, Ont., claiming damages for the confiscation of its property and reimbursement of its costs. (Source: CBC News, April 3, 3012). Trillium Power Wind Corp., a company that planned to build a series of huge wind farms in Lake Ontario sued the provincial government for $2.25-billion, claiming it unfairly cancelled all offshore wind projects earlier this year. (Source: The Globe and Mail, September 28, 2011)

The OPP was investigating allegations that government emails dealing with the $1.1-billion gas plants scandal were deliberately deleted in the dying days of former Liberal premier Dalton McGuinty's government. Also ongoing was the OPP probe into alleged financial irregularities at the ORNGE air ambulance service and potential breaches of a bribery section of the Election Act related to a 2015 by-election in Sudbury, Ontario. (Source: The Toronto Star, February 11, 2015)

As of September 2014, Ontario's debt was $304.4 billion, an amount that has more than doubled in the 12 years the McGuinty-Wynne Liberals were in office. The interest to carry that debt is $10.56 billion every year. And the Liberals plan to add another $26.7 billion to the debt with another three years of deficit spending. The Ontario Provincial Police's endorsement of the Liberals continues to hang over both organizations' heads. That endorsement came at a time when the police had open investigations into potential Liberal crimes (cancelling gas plants at a massive $1.1 billion public cost for partisan gain and deleting records about cancelling those gas plants). Only recently were three senior-ranking OPP officers (including one who was a Liberal candidate) suspended over shady dealings including fraud, breach of trust, and money laundering. The investigation that led to that arrest was conducted by the RCMP. (Source: Huffington Post, April 20, 2015)

In his book *Liars: The McGuinty-Wynne Record,* Daniel Dickin states that "...Ontario was Canada's reliable economic powerhouse, but that changed with the election of Dalton McGuinty's Liberals in 2003. Dalton McGuinty steered Ontario away from stability, prosperity, and responsible government into massive debt and deficit spending, constant tax increases, reckless government experiments and scandal after scandal - and then he lied about it all. His replacement, Kathleen Wynne, has followed the same path. Despite being elected on a platform of fresh promises in 2013, she has only continued the McGuinty legacy of scandals and lies".

On December 6, 2016, the Canadian Union of Public Employees filed a lawsuit against Ontario Premier Kathleen Wynne, Finance Minister Charles Sousa and former Energy Minister Bob Chiarelli for misfeasance over the sale of Hydro One. CUPE Ontario president Fred Hahn said the suit is aimed at stopping the sale of any more shares in the giant electricity transmission utility before private owners have control of its board. (Source: Canadian Press, December 7, 2016)

Here is another example of the game of politics. Ontario Premier Wynne was given a ceremonial robe known as a *siropa* during her visit in early 2016 to the Sikh Golden Temple in Amritsar, India. The temple's president, Avtar Singh Makkar, reportedly said that giving Premier Wynne the robe would be in violation of Sikh ethics which does not support pro-gay views and gay marriage. Premier Wynne supports same-sex marriage and is a lesbian. She generated front-page headlines in some Indian newspapers in 2016 for her visit to Amritsar's Golden

Temple. The big news there at the time was the Supreme Court's decision to examine the legality of a colonial-era law that treats homosexual relations as a criminal offence. (Source: *India Journal*, February 5, 2016)

Tax Havens

In April 2016, a huge leak of confidential documents has revealed how the rich and powerful use tax havens to hide their wealth. Eleven million documents were leaked from one of the world's most secretive companies, a Panamanian law firm called Mossack Fonseca. News media reports indicated the leaks show how Mossack Fonseca has helped clients launder money, dodge sanctions, and avoid tax. According to news reports, the company says it has operated beyond reproach for 40 years and has never been charged with criminal wrong-doing. The documents show 12 current or former heads of state, and at least 60 people, linked to current or former world leaders in the data. The authorities were determining which clients set up the accounts to evade taxes versus avoid taxes, as tax evasion is a criminal offence. The two founders of the Panamanian law firm Mossack Fonseca were arrested on February 9, 2017. Panamanian prosecutors raided the offices of Mossack Fonseca, the law firm at the center of the "Panama Papers" scandal, seeking possible links to Brazilian engineering company Odebrecht. Juergen Mossack and Ramon Fonseca, who is also a former adviser to Panama's president Juan Carlos Varela, were taken into custody by police in Panama. (Source: *CaribFlame*, February 10, 2017)

Prior to entering politics, Paul Martin became a wealthy man running his family business, Canada Steamship Lines (CSL), a Montreal based global shipping company. CSL had a complex offshore tax structure which allowed it to pay nominal Canadian corporate taxes since part of that structure included a subsidiary in Barbados which Canada has a tax treaty with. Under Canadian tax law, if one earns money offshore one cannot repatriate it without paying Canadian taxes. One way to get around this stipulation is to set up a subsidiary in an offshore haven which has a tax treaty with Canada. By doing this, one can bring home your overseas profits and pay minimal Canadian taxes. By 1994, however, these treaties were being abused by so many Canadian companies that Paul Martin was pressured as finance minister to plug them, which he did, except in the case of Barbados, where his family firm soon set up its subsidiary. According to Diane Francis "No self-respecting country in the world would do that." (Source: Why the offshore tax haven crisis won't get fixed, despite Panama Papers by Bruce Livesey, National Observer, April 4, 2016)

It is well known that some people chose to shelter their wealth, as evidenced by the following: In 2015, Rothschild & Co. paid a fine of $11.5 million to the U.S. Department of Justice, and avoided prosecution for helping Americans dodge taxes by using undeclared offshore accounts. Rothschild & Co. is among more than 80 Swiss banks who have paid about $80 billion to the U.S. government in penalties, fines, interest, and restitution. Recently, however, Rothschild is moving money in the reverse direction, by helping wealthy foreigners shelter their wealth in the U.S. through a trust company in Reno, Nevada. (Source: *Bloomberg Business Week* February 1-7, 2016)

Real Estate Agents

Beware of real estate sales representatives. The Real Estate Council of Ontario (RECO) is responsible for regulating real estate professionals in the province on behalf of the Ontario government. The RECO protects the public interest through a fair, safe, and informed marketplace. According to the Toronto Real Estate Board (TREB) statistics, about 42% of the real estate agents with the TREB sold less than six properties in 2015. I had entrusted a friend who was a real estate agent in Toronto, whom I had known since the 1980s, to find me a condo apartment unit to live in. I eventually purchased a few units through him and also listed for lease the condo units I was not living in. One of the units was in downtown Toronto where I had assumed the lease of the existing tenant, which the real estate agent collected every month and paid me by a certified cheque. The rent for this condo unit was $1,400 per month, including a locker and parking. I was unable to raise the rent by more than that allowed, due to rent controls. But what I eventually found out was that my long-time friend, and real estate agent, had held back $200 every month, which he pocketed for about one and a half years. When I confronted him with what I had found out, he apologized and returned the funds. According to information provided to me by another real estate broker, the real estate agent friend of mine had also inflated the price of the condo units I purchased through him, wherein the sale price favoured the seller, who is a lawyer and friend of his. Although I consulted a lawyer about this matter, I did not file a formal complaint with the Real Estate Council of Ontario because about two years had lapsed.

Developers

In 1987, I had purchased a pre-sale condo unit in The Residence of the World Trade Centre, at 10 Yonge Street. A large number of people had showed up to buy from the developer's plans. The developer was Camrost, whose founder was David Feldman. Mr. Feldman is presently the Founder, President and CEO of Camrost-Felcorp. He has been actively involved in the real estate business for reportedly over 40 years. The unit I purchased was going to be an investment which I intended to rent.

At the time of closing, the developer added the CMHC fee to the amount I owed, in spite of the fact that I had put down 25%. The CMHC premium applied only if a purchaser's down payment was less than 25% of the purchase price of a home. However, my lawyer advised me to close, and, thereafter, attempted to ask for a refund of the premium. A number of years later, I decided to contact Mr. Feldman, as a friend of mine knows Mr. Feldman and provided me with his telephone number. When I spoke to Mr. Feldman and asked him for a refund of my CMHC premium, he indicated that he was not prepared to provide the refund out of his own pocket. The former Camrost now goes by the restructured company name, Camrost-Felcorp.

Employers

The 1970s definitely was a different era in Ontario with respect to the overall working atmosphere, a lack of employment standards and environmental regulations, and a lack of proper conflict resolution between management and staff. Today, the working environment has changed somewhat due to workplace regulations that were introduced in 2000, namely the Employment Standards Act, and because of The Ontario Human Rights Code or the *longer reach*, or impact, of the Human Rights Commission.

Most employers have already consulted law firms that specialize in representing employers. Employers typically require employees to sign an employment agreement before an employee starts work, which usually tends to favour the employer. One example is when some employers offer the bare minimum with respect to benefits, such as severance. If an employee is terminated, many employers offer one week for each year of service, which is the bare minimum under the Employment Standards Act. If an employee had not signed an employment agreement, common law in Ontario would consider three critical factors: (1) an employee's age (2) length of service in the firm (3) position in that company. Consequently, an employee would be entitled to a significantly larger compensation, in the absence of an employment agreement, unless an employee was in a union, in which case the terms of the union would apply.

David Korten, author of *When Corporations Rule the World* (Berrett-Koehler Publishers), points the finger at the whole capitalist rat race. Advertisers get into the act by assuring us that their products can make us happy and whole again. So, many people go out and buy their products, which also allows them to keep up with the times, and that, of course, puts us right back at the beginning of the vicious cycle.

Multi-level Marketing

Multi-level marketing (MLM) is a marketing strategy in which the sales force is compensated, not only for sales they generate, but also for the sales of the other salespeople that they recruit. This recruited sales force is referred to as the participant's *downline*, and can provide multiple levels of compensation. Other terms used for MLM include pyramid selling, network marketing, and referral marketing (Source: Wikipedia). Many, if not all, of today's multilevel marketing programs involve some degree of fraud. Either they promise sales and incomes that can never be achieved, or they are nothing more than pyramid schemes, crudely disguised as multilevel marketing or MLM programs. When your profit derives from recruiting other people into the program, then you are involved in what's known as a pyramid scheme. This is bad in two ways.

Not only will you lose any funds you pour into this business, but it's illegal as well, and you could face steep fines, or worse. What's important to understand is that pyramid schemes always collapse in the end. No amount of fast talking will ever change that. Making money by signing up new members, who make money by signing up new members, is not a business plan with a future. (Source: Fraudguides.com)

It is truly amazing how many MLM companies exist in Canada. I remember Amway as being the notable one years ago, but the marketing ploys used by the new stock of MLM companies is staggering. What is even more horrible is that there are so many people that actually turn out for these events to be employed by them. Perhaps some hope that they will be successful and very wealthy in the MLM business, whereas others are intentionally recruited so they can build a pyramid scheme, or Ponzi scheme.

Psychopaths

Stefan Verstappen, writer, adventurer, martial artist, and street youth counselor, described the dangerous nature of psychopaths as people who lack "the ability to connect, in a positive way, with their fellow human beings." Among the attributes, ascribed to psychopaths by Verstappen, were an inability to feel empathy or remorse, as well as habitual lying and a lower fear threshold, which leads to increased risk-taking. Additionally, he contended that the smaller range of emotions possessed by psychopaths allows them to utilize more brain power to focus on manipulating others. While malevolent psychopaths, in the form of serial killers, receive a disproportionate amount of media coverage because their actions are gruesome and titillating, Verstappen warned that it is the ones who present themselves as *normal* within society that are particularly dangerous. To that end, such psychopaths seem to gravitate towards positions of power within government or business, and are often celebrated for their cunning machinations and risk-taking abilities. Beyond that, he noted that the idea of psychopaths infiltrating our institutions of power is such a difficult concept for people to accept or grasp, that it gives these devious individuals yet another advantage over the general population. According to author Douglas E. Richards, who has a master's degree in genetic engineering, and was Director of Biotechnology Licensing at Bristol-Myers Squibb, psychopaths can be incredibly charming, and often are brilliant liars and manipulators. "If they're caught in a lie, it doesn't faze them at all, because they don't have any shame, embarrassment, or self-consciousness, and will just create a bigger lie. They can even fool people who study them for a living, are cool as a cucumber under pressure, never take blame for anything, and have the ability to zero in on people's weaknesses."

Summary

The stock market is highly manipulated. It is not only my personal opinion and experience of losing lots of money in mutual funds and stocks. A friend of mine, Carlos Da Silva, is a venture capitalist and financier and has been in the financial industry for many years. He finally quit his job as a financial advisor as he could not continue to work in an industry where the clients were being intentionally mislead and almost always lost money. The commissions paid by the mutual fund companies to the investment advisors are substantial. Hence, there is a high level of motivation on the part of the advisors to continually sell these funds to their clients.

Many of the financial advisors operated under the premise of *buy and hold* for the long term. So they advised their clients to *buy and hold* their funds, with a periodic review. They further believed investors should stick to no-load funds, buy load funds without the load through a discount broker and a back-end load. A back-end-load is a fee (sales charge or load) that investors pay when selling mutual fund shares within a specified number of years, usually five to ten years. The fee amounts to a percentage of the value of the share being sold and is highest in the first year, and decreases yearly until the specified holding period ends, at which time it drops to zero.

The many people in the various professions mentioned in this chapter are Christians, and/or religious, but choose to ignore religion when making the type of business decisions they have carried out for the benefit of themselves and their corporations. One such example is the cigarette manufacturers who produce a substance that is known to contribute to serious health problems. Similarly, financial advisors intentionally sold mutual funds that declined in value or did not produce high positive returns that were always displayed in big printed ads in many Toronto newspapers and elsewhere.

The Economist's Britain correspondent, Tom Wainwright, and former Mexico correspondent, found that there was a parallel between the $300 billion illegal drug business and the corporate world. The drug cartels donate to churches and various charitable causes; they keep people from various segments of society employed in the drug business, including some police and government officials, thereby solidifying their position to deal in drugs.

Sources: Wikipedia – United States Campaign Finance Controversy; *Toronto Star*, December 22, 2012; *National Post*, March 8, 2016; *BBC News*, April 4, 2016

CHAPTER 8

The New World Order

Organized Crime

An Ontario mafia expert told a Quebec corruption probe, in September 2012, that York Regional Police may be investigating government contracts awarded to organized crime groups, according to Allan Woods of the Quebec Bureau of the *Toronto Star*. The issue of rigged government contracts had rocked the provincial and municipal governments in Quebec, and was the subject of a public inquiry into the infiltration of, and corruption of, the province's construction industry, its unions, and the public officials who dole out lucrative contracts. It was the most concrete example that emerged of the links that exist between the activities of Italian mafia groups in Quebec and Ontario. A joint investigation by the *Toronto Star* and *Radio-Canada*, in September 2012, had revealed the rise of the 'Ndrangheta, or the *Calabrian mafia*, which the RCMP has listed as one of its *tier 1* threats in the Greater Toronto Area (GTA) because of its tremendous influence economically, and because its power base is in the GTA. The 'Ndrangheta is one of three separate mafia clans active in Canada; the other two are the Cosa Nostra, or Sicilian mafia, and the Camorra, originally from Naples. Part of the reason they are so powerful is because of their economic influence and pervasiveness. The RCMP estimates that the Calabrian mafia has seven Canadian *locali*, or cells, most of which are based in the GTA, and that they have seen no evidence of political corruption, unlike the large-scale corruptions that have rocked Italy.

Although the mafia have a lower profile in Ontario compared to Quebec, they are more active in Ontario. Some people, including professionals, are naive or uninformed, and fall prey to the mafia, as they do not realize the extent of their influence. They have a wide swath of influence which includes political figures, law enforcement, people in the criminal justice system, and the manufacturing industries. Former Premier Dalton McGuinty said he had never received warnings from police or other authorities about organized crime infiltrating Ontario politics, and doubted the accusations were true. He claimed the first time he had heard about this was through the media, and indicated that if there were warranted allegations, they should be made in a substantive way.

In 2011, the Quebec government launched the Charbonneau commission to probe the ways the Cosa Nostra and outlaw biker gangs have infiltrated Quebec's $50-billion construction industry. Several arrests followed, including construction magnate Tony Accurso, and confidants of Montreal Mayor, Gerald Tremblay. The probe findings resulted in the creation of a provincial anti-corruption police squad, which issued search warrants of public-private partnerships to build a mega hospital affiliated with McGill University.

Mafia activities in Ontario tend to fly under the radar of the public and the police, according to York Regional Police Detective, Mike Amato (now retired). One of the reasons is that the 'Ndrangheta is hard for police to infiltrate and arrest because it operates along strict blood lines, namely one is either born or

Sources: *Toronto Star*, September 19, 2012 and September 21, 2012; *CTV News,* September 20, 2012; *CBC News*, September 20, 2012

marries into the clan. They are integrated into the community and in a variety of business positions such as bankers, accountants, limousine drivers, lawyers, and entrepreneurs. They operate under a strict code where only "family" are trusted, and all others must be manipulated for financial gain. The Ontario government, however, has made significant investments in the fight against organized crime.

A *Toronto Star* article dated August 5, 2010, indicates that the OPP stated that Ontario government employees, and employees of two private companies, received cash, free services, and electronics, in exchange for awarding businesses. The OPP's anti-rackets branch investigated irregular transactions between a vendor-of-record and employees of the Ministry of Transportation, Ministry of Economic Development and Trade, and Ministry of Community and Social Services, as well as two facility management companies. An overview of the investigation, filed in the Ontario Court of Justice, identifies the companies as SNC Lavalin Profac, and CB Richard Ellis, two companies contracted by the government to manage facilities. In some instances, the invoices were false, in that no work was actually done; in other instances, the dollar value of the invoices was inflated; and in another case, employees disclosed the amounts of bids from competitors to a vendor. The OPP has investigated inappropriate procurement practices of a former employee of the Ontario Realty Corporation.

My tenure with the provincial government did not involve undertaking real estate deals with criminal organizations. However, during an appraisal assignment in the private sector, I met a property owner in the GTA who amassed well over $100 million worth in real estate in Ontario, and is reported to be affiliated with the mafia.

The Rise of Corruption

In ancient times, the policies of Rome regarding its trading partners in the East, concerning the value of gold and silver bullion, strongly indicate manipulation at both ends of the trading routes, which ultimately favoured any class that controlled bullion supplies.

Before WW II, there were three prominent Americans who were instrumental in funding the Nazis, namely John J. McCloy, Chairman of National City Bank (now Citicorp); Allen Dulles and his brother John Foster Dulles of Schroeder Bank; and Prescott Bush, a director at Union Banking Corporation and the Hamburg American shipping line. Following World War II, John McCloy became the high commissioner of occupied Germany; John Foster Dulles became President Eisenhower's secretary of state; Allan Dulles became the longest-serving CIA director; and Prescott Bush was mainly responsible for starting the CIA. John McCloy and Allan Dulles were a part of the Warren Commission (which is now discredited) assigned by President Lyndon B. Johnson to investigate the assassination of President John F. Kennedy. (Source: *The Trillion-Dollar Conspiracy* by Jim Marrs – HarperCollins Publishers, 2010).

Corruption had been booming in Latin America in the 1990s. The 20-year career of former Venezuelan President, Carlos Andres Perez, was abruptly ended in May 1993, when the Supreme Court indicted him for allegedly misusing US $17.2 million, from a secret fund. The first time an impeachment, in Latin America, of a leader, took place when former President Fernando Collor de Mello, of Brazil, was impeached by the Brazilian Senate in September 1992, for collecting hundreds of millions of dollars from an extortion ring. No president had ever been impeached for corruption in Brazil, or elsewhere in Latin America, prior to that. A second impeachment occurred in Latin

America in May 2016, when President Dilma Rousseff was impeached by the Brazilian Senate. President Rousseff is accused of *pedaladas fiscais*, creative accounting techniques, which hid some 26 billion dollars of debt incurred by her government's social programs. Cooking the books may have allowed her to be re-elected in 2014 by a slight margin, but it has also contributed to the reduction of the country's credit rating to near junk levels. Brazil is mired in its worst recession since the 1930s. (Sources: *The Globe and Mail,* March 4, 2016; *American Thinker, "Brazil's Impeachment of President Dilma and America's Hillary Dilema"* by Vernon Roken, May 8, 2016)

Four mayors of Latin American capitals, namely Bogota, Buenos Aires, Caracas and Panama City, were forced to leave office because of corruption charges.

The above examples are only part of well publicized cases across the region. Eight former leaders of Latin American countries were investigated or convicted for corruption, namely Callor de Mello, of Brazil, Carlos Andres Perez, and Jamie Lusinchi, of Venezuela, Luis Alberto Monge, of Costa Rica, Salvador Jorge Blanco, of the Dominican Republic, Luis Garcia Meza of Bolivia, and Manuel Solis Palma, of Panama.

General Manuel Antonio Noriega, former de facto leader of Panama, was under indictment and served a United States sanctioned prison sentence. Noriega's U.S. prison sentence ended in September 2007, pending the outcome of extradition requests by both Panama and France, for convictions in absentia for murder in 1995, and money laundering in 1999. France was granted its extradition request in April 2010. He arrived in Paris on April 27, 2010, and after a re-trial as a condition of the extradition, he was found guilty and sentenced to seven years in jail, in July 2010. A conditional release was granted on September 23, 2011, for Noriega to be extradited to serve 20 years in Panama. He returned to Panama on December 11, 2011. (Source: Wikipedia)

In a number of cases, politicians have used corruption charges to wound their enemies, or as a pretext to gain favour with the public. Many of the politicians, who denounce their fellow colleagues, are corrupt themselves. In some countries, it is almost impossible to hold a prominent office without taking part in corruption. Civilian governments have deep roots in Latin American societies, and corruption scandals have caused instability in the economy of those countries. But corruption is not restricted to Latin America alone. Corruption exists in the United States, Canada, Europe, Africa, Russia, and Asia, including India and China. Akaash Maharaj, Chief Executive Officer of the Global Organization of Parliamentarians Against Corruption, said the following in his address to the United Nations (Source: GOPAC 2014-2015 Annual Report):

"The UN Development Program now estimates that the developing world loses €10 to corruption for every €1 it receives in official aid. GOPAC estimates that corruption now kills more people than war and famine combined. And the UN's new Sustainable Development Goals now include Goal 16, which acknowledges that nations must combat corruption as a precondition to achieving social and economic development."

The annual release of the global Corruption Perceptions Index (CPI) is rarely good news for Latin America, except for a handful of standout nations. Published every year since 1995, by Transparency International, the CPI compiles results from independent surveys by Non-Government Organizations to estimate how corrupt the public sectors of different countries are. Essentially, the statistics mark a failure to effectively address corruption in Latin America over almost two decades. Canada ranks ninth in the list of countries with the least CPI.

New World Order

Proponents say the New World Order (NWO) is an anticipated new era of global cooperation between nations and cultures, aimed at providing much of the earth's population with a number of things they need.

According to author and media analyst Mike Dice, "Detractors of the NWO claim it's the systematic take-over by secret societies, quasi-government entities, and corporations who are covertly organizing a global socialist all-powerful government which aims to regulate every aspect of people's lives, rendering them a perpetual working-class while the elite leadership lives in luxury." Mark Dice argues that the New World Order secret societies, such as the Illuminati, Bilderberg Group, Skull and Bones, and Bohemian Grove, direct human affairs and global politics, mainly those of the United States. Dice believes the Illuminati secret society represents the pinnacle of power in politics, banking, and the news media, as well as in the entertainment industry. Dice indicates Hollywood's elite studios, producers, and celebrities have a secret agenda and are part of a covert conspiracy where they use celebrities and entertainment as a powerful propaganda tool to shape our culture, attitudes, and behaviors, and to promote corrupt government policies and programs.

According to Dr. Henry Makow, Ph.D., the New World Order is an attempt to overthrow God, and replace Him with Satan. The essence of today's political struggle is spiritual, a cosmic battle between God or good, and Satan or evil, for the soul of humans. The struggle is between an international financial elite, led by the Illuminati, and the remnants of humanity that still uphold God's plan. The plan by the elite is to remake this planet as its private neo feudal preserve by reducing the world's population through plague, catastrophe or war, and mind control, and breeding of the remaining population as serfs. Essentially, the NWO aims to say black is white and evil is good. It creates a bogus reality designed to serve the few and enslave the many. Dr. Makow indicates that no one today should be blamed for the crucifixion of Christ; instead, we should be responsible for what we do to upset the spiritual order that Christ represented and what may be considered the order that exists in the universe, or, more particularly, on earth.

As the President Kennedy assassination, and 9-11, prove, the US, and most countries, have been totally subverted by a Luciferian international criminal elite. The role of politicians, media, and education, is to keep the public deluded and distracted while the elite steadily advances its goal of world tyranny. In essence, western society can be regarded as a massive fraud that has been orchestrated against the unsuspecting public. Most people are distracted, unaware or unwilling to accept the existence of a powerful group that has an elite plan for the world. They either roll their eyes or move on in disbelief. And that is exactly why the elite's plan has succeeded and become more repressive over the years and moved in the direction of a police state. The plan has been aided by the mass media (through mind control) which is owned and controlled by the Illuminati.

The Illuminati also use bribes of money and sex to gain control of people in high places, and then blackmail them with the threat of financial ruin, public exposure, or assassination (such as the President Kennedy assassination). Americans have often been intentionally mislead, and even clearly lied to, about important events that changed history. This includes the President Kennedy assassination, which was a government cover-up, as opined by Mark Lane and the former Governor of Minnesota, Jesse Ventura. An attorney in the U.S., Mark Lane, concluded that the CIA plotted the murder of former President John F. Kennedy. Mark Lane, who personally knew President Kennedy, immediately became suspicious of the claims that Oswald acted alone.

The Zapruder film shows a bullet striking JFK from behind, and the same film shows a piece of President Kennedy's skull being blown off by another bullet that came from another side of the President's limousine. In Mr. Lane's interview with witness Jean Hill, she suggested that the fatal gunshot came from a *grassy knoll* on Dealey Plaza. The CIA was known for planning the assassinations of heads of state; it had, according to former President Truman, "become a danger to America." President John F. Kennedy, and his brother Robert Kennedy, were planning on disbanding the CIA, before JFK was killed, and subsequently, his brother Robert Kennedy. According to Mark Lane, the CIA functions as a fourth branch of government, operates without oversight, and is actually more powerful than the other branches.

The book "Mary's Mosaic" by Peter Janney will introduce the reader to a crucial new aspect of the Kennedy presidency. Perhaps the most chilling aspect of that book is the detailed and convincing manner in which it reveals the power of the official JFK assassination cover-up imposed by the U.S. government immediately after his death and the power to manipulate the media and to steal documents; the willingness to manipulate the judicial system by aggressively attempting to frame an innocent man for a crime he did not commit; and even the willingness to commit murder to silence a citizen, namely Mary Myer, who was about to publicly oppose the sham conclusions of the Warren Commission Report. These comments were made by Douglas P. Horne, Chief Analyst for Military Records, The Assassination Records Review Board (ARRB) and author of Inside the

Assassination Records Review Board: The U.S. Government's Final Attempt to Reconcile the Conflicting Medical Evidence in the Assassination of JFK., Vols. I-V.

The freemasons created America as an effective base for their world-encompassing activities and to attain their utmost aim of world supremacy. One of the means of the Illuminati accomplishing their goals is through politicians who often betray the public for fame and fortune. The actions taken by politicians across the globe, such as free-trade, mass immigration etc., has channeled the public in the direction favoured by the Illuminati. Many best-selling authors believe the political, cultural, and economic elite have either been duped, or are willing agents of a huge conspiracy, and that human beings have taken a turn in the wrong direction. The only way things can be turned around is if the majority of the population takes appropriate action.

The Jewish Conspiracy and the New World Order

In circa 1770, a syndicate of bankers, led by Mayer Rothschild, started the Illuminati, a cult designed to subvert society. The goals of the Illuminati were the destruction of Christianity, monarchies, nation-states, the abolition of family ties and marriage by means of promoting homosexuality and promiscuity, the end of inheritance and private property, and the suppression of any collective identity in the spurious name of universal human brotherhood or diversity. The Illuminati favour a world government, or internationalism.

The *secret society* for Judaism, as well as Freemasonry, Zionism and Communism, adopted an organizational model that now applies to the whole world. Essentially, the leadership deceives and manipulates the membership with idealistic-sounding goals. Only those corruptible are let in on the true agenda and allowed to rise, and, in so doing, have often accepted the devil's bargain. Most Jews are unaware that Judaism largely eschews the Old Testament in favour of the Talmud and Cabala. These books are full of hate and contempt for non-Jews. The Cabala is the basis of modern witchcraft, astrology, numerology, tarot cards, black magic, androgyny, sex worship (which has engulfed the world), and much of the New Age movement. It teaches that good and evil are one, or that black is white, and vice-versa. The main reason for anti-Semitism is that Judaism contains an ideology of supremacy and domination. The Illuminati Jewish leadership regards itself as God.

In extreme cases, like the Rothschild's, their quest for limitless wealth and power, their need to own and control everything, defines Satan's domination. Thus, organized Jewery, through its Freemasonic arm, has sabotaged personal and social identity based on race, religion, nation, and family. They have caused revolution, division, corruption, and wars like Iraq and Afghanistan, with the potential for causing World War 3, as well as having sought to normalize dysfunction and deviance. All this is to prove that the salutary and natural order represented by Christian ideals is corrupt and hypocritical, and must be replaced by Jewish gods, namely communism, socialism, and their latest utopian test tube tyranny – the New World Order.

Fatal Results of Supporting State Issued Debt-Free Money

Historical incidences point overwhelmingly to the fatal results when a leader, or a state, has attempted to support the principle of state-issued money as credit, which mobilizes the international bankster class in areas where they have control. The banksters make war against such a *breakaway* leader, or state, or, alternatively, the leader of a state advocating such policies is murdered, with a consistency that belies mere coincidence. The following examples reference this critical point:

- The manipulation of the collapse of the issuances of the US Congress during the 1780s by a return to the gold or bullion standard, which greatly contracted the American money supply, causing a depression.
- The assassination of President Abraham Lincoln for issuing debt-free Greenbacks to finance the northern effort during the American War between the States, and the subsequent National Currency Act.
- The assassination of President James Garfield, mere months into his presidency, after he had suggested his willingness to return to state-created, and issued, debt-free money.
- The manipulation of the American money supply prior to, and during, the Great Depression, first by vastly expanding credit, and then vastly contracting the money supply.
- Some researchers have indicated that the war against Nazi Germany had a secret purpose for the banking elite of the West, who having aided Adolf Hitler's and the Nazis' rise to power, were quickly alarmed by Nazi Germany's deliberate moves to restore state-issued debt-free money, and Germany's efforts to explore alternative paradigms of physics that would lead Germany to energy independence and self-sufficiency.
- President John F. Kennedy was murdered five months after his issuance of an executive order authorizing the U.S. Treasury to print $4 billion worth of debt-free U.S. Notes, bypassing the privately owned and controlled Federal Reserve Bank completely.

Sources: *Illuminati - The Cult That Hijacked The World* by Henry Makow Ph.D – Silas Green, Publisher 2011; *Babylon's Banksters* by Joseph P. Farrell - Feral House, Publisher, 2010; *The Trillion-Dollar Conspiracy* by Jim Marrs - HarperCollins Publishers, 2010

Love Canal Incident

Love Canal is an area in Niagara Falls, New York, located in the LaSalle section of Niagara Falls. It officially covers 36 square blocks in the far southeastern corner of the city, along 99th Street and Read Avenue. Two bodies of water define the neighborhood: Bergholtz Creek to the north, and the Niagara River one-quarter mile to the south. Hooker Chemical deeded the site to the Niagara Falls School Board in 1953, for a dollar, with a liability limitation clause. Long after having taken control of the land, the School Board proceeded to have it developed, including construction activity that substantially breached containment structures in a number of ways, allowing previously trapped chemicals to seep out. The resulting breaches, combined with particularly heavy rainstorms, released and spread the chemical waste, leading to a public health emergency and an urban planning scandal. In what became a test case for liability clauses, Hooker Chemical was found to be negligent in their disposal of waste, though not reckless in the sale of the land. The dumpsite was discovered and investigated by the local newspaper, the *Niagara Falls Gazette*, from 1976 through the evacuation in 1978. By the mid-1970s, Love Canal became the subject of national and international attention after it was revealed in the press that the site had formerly been used to bury 22,000 tons of toxic waste by Hooker Chemical Company (now Occidental Petroleum).

Many lawsuits were filed, and Hooker Chemical was sued reportedly for more than $11 billion. The corporation denied its involvement, even when reportedly faced by the Federal Justice Department in 1979, and New York State in 1989. The environmental disaster involved toxins which affected industrial workers stricken by nervous disorders and cancers, to the discovery of toxic materials in the milk of nursing mothers. Agencies at the state and federal levels spent hundreds of millions of dollars trying to clean up the pollution. Of that, Hooker Chemical has eventually been persuaded to contribute about $130 million. (Source: Wikipedia)

Tobacco Companies and the Catastrophic Health Effects of Smoking

Another massive fraud is the one that was played by the tobacco manufacturers on the world. It is appropriately depicted in a movie called *The Insider,* with Al Pacino and Russell Crowe, which recounts the chain of events that pitted a man against the tobacco industry, and dragged two people into the fight of their lives. Crowe plays Dr. Jeffery Wigand, an executive at the cigarette manufacturer Brown & Williamson, who is fired by his employer. He decides to become a paid consultant for a *60 Minutes* producer who was working on alleged unethical practices in the tobacco industry. The movie shows that corporate America will pursue all legal means to save a billion dollar industry and a habit of a segment of the population.

Tobacco was first used by the peoples of the pre-Columbian Americas. Native Americans cultivated the tobacco plant and smoked it in pipes for medicinal and ceremonial purposes. Most Europeans didn't get their first taste of tobacco until the mid-16th century, when adventurers and diplomats like France's Jean Nicot, for whom nicotine is named, began to popularize its use. The first successful commercial tobacco crop was cultivated in Virginia, in 1612, by Englishman John Rolfe. Within seven years, it was the colony's largest export. Over the next two centuries, the growth of tobacco, as a cash crop fueled the demand in North America for slave labor. (Source: CNN – "A Brief History of Tobacco")

In 1950, Richard Doll published research in the *British Medical Journal* showing a close link between smoking and lung cancer. Four years later, in 1954, the British Doctors Study, a study of some 40,000 doctors over 20 years, confirmed the suggestion, based on which the government issued advice that smoking and lung cancer rates were related. On January 11, 1964, the United States *Surgeon General's Report on Smoking and Health* was published; this led millions of American smokers to quit, and resulted in the banning of certain advertising, and the requirement of warning labels on tobacco products. (Source: Wikipedia)

In the early 1990s, the tobacco companies indicated that there was no correlation between smoking and cancer. One can see how arrogant the establishments truly were – as most executives of the tobacco manufacturers sent their attorneys to testify before the US Congress, wherein they claimed there were no health effects from smoking cigarettes. As more and more medical studies were published, and the surgeon general's warning was issued, a caution was posted on all cigarette packets – that smoking causes lung cancer.

But one of the biggest blows to the tobacco companies was when the individual states in the US commenced legal action after incurring huge health care costs for treating people with health problems related to the effects of smoking.

As smoking prevalence rates have declined in the traditional markets of North America and Western Europe, the tobacco industry has re-focused its promotional efforts onto the less developed and emerging nations in Africa, Asia, the Middle East, the former Soviet Union, and Latin America. The often weak regulatory environment in these countries has further encouraged the industry to target those populations. If current patterns continue, tobacco use is projected to kill approximately 10 million people, every year, throughout the world, by 2020. Most (approximately 70%) of these deaths are expected to occur in less developed and emerging nations. (Source: Cancer Council, NSW, Australia)

Pollution Caused by Big Oil: Chevron Case

One example of the pollution and its impact by an oil company is the Chevron incident in Ecuador. Between 1964 and 1990, U.S. oil giant, Texaco (now Chevron), contaminated Ecuador's Amazon rainforest by dumping 80,000 tons of oil and toxic residues, thereby ruining rivers and drinking water in a 19,305 square mile area, and contributing to high cancer rates and birth defects among the local population. The villagers' original lawsuit was filed against Texaco Inc. in 1993, and Chevron inherited the lawsuit when it merged with Texaco in 2001.

According to writer/activist Mitch Anderson, "Over the course of more than two decades of operations, Chevron abandoned more than 900 unlined waste pits, gouged out of the jungle floor, that leached toxins into soils and streams; contaminated the air by burning the waste pits; dumped oil along roads; and spilled millions of gallons of pure crude from ruptured pipelines. Internal company documents demonstrate that Chevron officials ordered field workers to destroy records of oil spills. The company refused to develop an environmental response plan or pipeline maintenance program, and Chevron never conducted a single health evaluation or environmental impact study despite the obvious harm it was causing." (Source: Mitch Anderson, "Chevron Found Guilty in Amazon Pollution Case," sfgate.com – February 16, 2011).

Huffington Post reported that by 2013, "over 1,400 have died, and thousands more (Ecuadorians) have suffered illnesses" resulting from the severe contamination in the region.

Writing for the Canadian website, rabble.ca, Raluca Bejan, and Santiago Escobar, called the situation *the Amazonian Chernobyl,* and stated: "In 2011, an Ecuadorian court ruled for Chevron having to pay $9.5 billion dollars for the destruction it has caused." But, by then, Chevron already liquidated all of its owned assets in Ecuador. Ecuador's indigenous people were left with no other choice but to pursue Chevron's resources globally. Having filed a lawsuit in the US, the Ecuadorian villagers have also filed similar lawsuits against Chevron in Argentina and Brazil.

In 2012, *Canadian Press* reported that the villagers planned to file lawsuits in "30 countries, on four continents, where Chevron has assets" in order to collect the damages owed. Bejan and Escobar stressed that "This is a transnational justice case. If a global world allows Chevron to operate globally, to pick and choose its countries of interest, to pack up and leave when convenient, social responsibility should also be demanded across national borders . . ."In a boost to Ecuadorean villagers' long-running bid to enforce a $9.5 billion judgment against Chevron Corp., the highest court in Canada, on September 5, 2015, ruled that villagers could move forward with an effort to seize assets tied to Chevron. The ruling in Canada was part of a broader legal battle between Ecuadorean farmers and Chevron that has stretched for more than two decades and been litigated across multiple continents. Originally, Texaco Inc. was accused by Ecuadorean farmers of polluting the Amazon rain forest with its oil drilling. Chevron denied liability for the environmental damage.

An Ecuadorean court in 2011 had awarded $19 billion to the plaintiffs, one of the largest environmental verdicts in history, which was ultimately reduced in 2013 to $9.5 billion by Ecuador's highest court. Chevron has refused to pay the judgment and embarked on an aggressive legal effort to undermine it.

As Chevron doesn't hold any assets in Ecuador, Steven Donziger, the primary lawyer, had originally spearheaded the plaintiffs' efforts, and his team had tried to enforce the judgment by going after Chevron's assets around the world, including Canada, Brazil and Argentina.

Since 2011, Alan Lenczner has been the lead Canadian lawyer for Ecuadorian plaintiffs, attempting to access Chevron assets outside Ecuador, given the dearth of company assets in Canada. Alan Lenczner is a founding partner of the Toronto law firm Lenczner Slaght, where he is counsel for Yaiguaje et al., the Ecuadorian plaintiffs seeking to sue Chevron Canada following a US $18.3 billion judgment in 2001, obtained in Ecuador against its parent company, Chevron, for oil pollution in the Amazon. Lenczner was up against Benjamin Zarnett of Goodmans LLP, and Clarke Hunter of Norton Rose Fulbright Canada. According to the *Financial Post*, Zarnett and Hunter "argued that enforcing the Ecuadorian judgment in Ontario would be impossible because Chevron's corporate structure is too complicated. Chevron is structured sort of like a Russian nesting doll: The Canadian subsidiary is owned by another Chevron-subsidiary, which is owned by another subsidiary, and so on. There are no fewer than seven corporate layers separating the Canadian unit from Chevron Corp." The ruling weakens the so-called *corporate veil* that has shielded subsidiaries from responsibility for the actions of their corporate parents.

John Perkins experienced firsthand the deceitful and destructive practices employed by oil companies and government agencies, and the negative impacts on the environments and cultures of the locals in the Ecuadoran Amazon. Mr. Perkins was an Economic Hit Man (EHM). EHMs are highly paid professionals hired by the U.S. government, or one of its agencies, to cheat countries around the world out of trillions of dollars.

Money is loaned from the World Bank, the U.S. Agency for International Development, and other similar organizations, for various developments in foreign countries, according to John Perkins. The loans benefit mainly U.S. corporations who use natural resources and the control of the same to complete the developments. This leaves some countries with very significant debts which they are incapable of paying. As per Mr. Perkins, these corporations have tools which include fraudulent financial reports, rigged elections, extortion, payoffs, sex, and murder. (Source: *Confessions of an Economic Hit Man* by John Perkins – Penguin Group Publishing, 2004)

Three Worst Nuclear Meltdowns

The three most disastrous meltdowns were Three Mile Island (TMI) in Pennsylvania, Chernobal in Ukraine, and Fukushima in Japan. The Three Mile Island accident was a partial nuclear meltdown that occurred on March 28, 1979, in reactor number two, of the Three Mile Island Nuclear Generating Station (TMI-2), in Dauphin County, Pennsylvania, United States. It was the worst accident in U.S. commercial nuclear power plant history. The incident was rated a five on the seven-point International Nuclear Event Scale.

A cleanup started in August 1979, and officially ended in December 1993, with a total cleanup cost of about $1 billion.

The accident at the TMI plant occurred twelve days after the release of the movie, *The China Syndrome*. In the film, television reporter Kimberly Wells (Jane Fonda), and her cameraman, Richard Adams (Michael Douglas), secretly filmed a major accident at a nuclear power plant while taping a series on nuclear power. Plant supervisor, Jack Godell (Jack Lemmon), discovers potentially catastrophic safety violations at the plant, and, with Wells' assistance, attempts to raise public awareness of these violations. After the release of the film, Jane Fonda began lobbying against nuclear power. In an attempt to counter her efforts, the then elderly Edward Teller, a nuclear physicist and long-time government science adviser, best known for contributing to the Teller-Ulam design breakthrough that made *hydrogen bombs* possible, personally lobbied in favour of nuclear power. (Source: Wikipedia)

The Chernobyl disaster was a catastrophic nuclear accident that occurred on April 26, 1986, at the Chernobyl Nuclear Power Plant in the city of Pripyat, then located in the Ukrainian Soviet Socialist Republic of the Soviet Union (USSR). An explosion and fire released large quantities of radioactive particles into the atmosphere, which spread over much of the western USSR and Europe. The Chernobyl disaster was the worst nuclear power plant accident in history, in terms of cost and casualties. It is one of only two classified as a level seven event (the maximum classification) on the International Nuclear Event Scale, the other being the Fukushima Daiichi nuclear disaster in Japan, in 2011. The struggle to contain the contamination, and avert a greater catastrophe, ultimately involved over 500,000 workers, and cost an estimated 18 billion rubles. During the accident, 31 people died, and long-term effects, such as cancers, are still being investigated. (Source: Wikipedia)

The Fukushima Daiichi nuclear disaster was an energy accident at the Fukushima I Nuclear Power Plant in Fukushima, initiated primarily by the tsunami following the Tōhoku earthquake on March 11, 2011. Immediately after the earthquake, the active reactors automatically shut down their sustained fission reactions. However, the tsunami destroyed the emergency generators cooling the reactors, causing reactor number four to overheat from the decay heat, from the fuel rods. The insufficient cooling led to three nuclear meltdowns and the release of radioactive material, beginning on March 12, 2011. Several hydrogen-air chemical explosions occurred between March 12 and March 15, 2011. On July 5, 2012, the Fukushima Nuclear Accident Independent Investigation Commission (NAIIC) found that the causes of the accident had been foreseeable, and that the plant operator, Tokyo Electric Power Company (TEPCO), had failed to meet basic safety requirements such as risk assessment, preparing for containing collateral damage, and developing evacuation plans. On October 12, 2012, TEPCO admitted, for the first time, that it had failed to take necessary measures for fear of inviting lawsuits or protests against its nuclear plants. (Source: Wikipedia)

The ongoing debacle of the Fukushima disaster includes background radiation rising, food chain contamination, and the targeting of whistleblowers. Conditions are far worse in Japan than the media is letting on, and the government there has placed a gag order, such that whistleblowers can go to jail if they reveal information about the dire situation. Further, doctors who submit a diagnosis of radiation poisoning from Fukushima victims, won't get paid by the government. "The truth of the matter is that the health effects are horrendous, but we'll never know how bad they are because the government is obliterating any long term medical records," according to Matthew Stein, bestselling author, engineer, designer, and green builder.

New rules, from the Canadian Nuclear Safety Commission, dictate that iodine thyroid-blocking pills must be delivered to homes and workplaces, near nuclear plants, by the end of 2015. (Sources: Wikipedia; DurhamRegion.com, October 14, 2014)

According to Matthew Stein, America is facing the same dangers that the Fukushima disaster brought to light, as many of its nuclear plants are either in flood zones or on fault lines. Additionally, many of America's nuclear facilities have gone past their life span of 40 years, and need to undergo a very expensive decommissioning process. Matthew Stein has stated accounts of brave whistleblowers in America's nuclear industry, and the negative consequences that *doing the right thing* had on their lives and careers.

Genetically Modified Organisms and Food

A genetically modified organism (GMO) is the by-product of splicing a gene from one species into the DNA of another. Genetically modified foods, or genetically engineered foods, are foods produced from organisms that have had changes introduced into their DNA, using the methods of genetic engineering. Genetic engineering techniques allow for the introduction of new traits, as well as greater control over traits than previous methods had.

Genetically modified potatoes sold in the U.S. have had their DNA spliced with a gene from a soil bacterium similar to Bacillus anthrax. The added gene results in potatoes creating their own pesticide called Bacillus thuringiensis toxin, or Bt, which kills insects that consume a GM potato. The same Bt genes have also been placed into the DNA of corn and cottonseed. Bt is classified as a pesticide by the Environmental Protection Agency (EPA).

Commercial sale of genetically modified foods began in 1994, when Calgene first marketed its unsuccessful Flavr Savr delayed-ripening tomato. Most GMOs have primarily focused on cash crops in high demand by farmers such as soybean, corn, and canola. The *Big 6* pesticide and GMO corporations are

BASF, Bayer, Dupont, Dow Chemical Company, Monsanto, and Syngenta. They dominate the agricultural input market, as they own the world's seed, pesticide, and biotechnology industries. Some GM seeds are subject to intellectual property rights owned by corporations.

According to the United Nations Conference on Trade and Development (UNCTAD), corporate concentration of the agricultural input market "has far-reaching implications for global food security, as the privatization and patenting of agricultural innovation (gene traits, transformation technologies and seed germplasm) has been supplanting traditional agricultural understandings of seed, farmers' rights, and breeders' rights." Corporations that created chemical warfare in the 1980s, transformed it to agrichemicals, which is the continuation of chemical warfare in our food system. Now corporations have an opportunity to lay claim to owning life by pretending to be inventors. It appears GMO, to them, actually means "God, Move Over." Corporations created the seed, own the seed, have a right to rent collection from life, and they got this into the international treaty.

Arthur Anderson Consulting Group was responsible for helping Monsanto create a master plan for a few corporations that were determined to control the world's food supply by ensuring that 100% of all commercial seeds were genetically modified and patented. Their plan was to quickly implement the technology worldwide, before resistance could interfere, and to flood the marketplace with GMO food, so nothing could be done and people would just surrender. These corporations regard their plan as good business, even though many people regard their position as arrogant and a dangerous disrespect for nature. It is reported that Monsanto has, to a large extent, achieved control of GMOs since certain key employees have moved to the FDA, which has ensured Monsanto's decisions are implemented.

Monsanto controls reportedly 85% of all genetically engineered germplasm.

On March 26, 2013, President Barack Obama inked his name to H.R. 933, a continuing resolution spending bill approved in Congress days earlier. Buried deep within the bill exists a provision that grossly protects biotech corporations such as Monsanto from litigation (Source: RT, March 28, 2013). The said bill effectively bars federal courts from being able to halt the sale or planting of GMO, or GE, crops and seeds, no matter what health consequences from the consumption of these products may come to light in the future.

The said bill was written in part by the very billion-dollar corporation that will benefit directly from the legislation. According to an article published in the *New York Daily News*, U.S. Sen. Roy Blunt (R-Missouri) "worked with Monsanto to craft the language in the bill." Sen. Roy Blunt received $64,250 from Monsanto to go towards his campaign committee between 2008 and 2012. The Money Monocle website adds that Blunt has been the largest Republican Party recipient of Monsanto funding as of late. (Source: RT, March 28, 2013)

Some hold the view that food from genetically modified crops are not inherently riskier to human health than conventional food. In his book, *Seeds of Deception,* Jeffrey M. Smith has exposed industry for rigging research, covering up alarming evidence of health dangers, and applying political pressure. He shows how sound science has allowed dangerous, genetically engineered food into the public's diet, and how the public has been duped and marginalized, as well as how a few corporations, led by Monsanto, have turned the public into guinea pigs.

GMOs in Canada have been allowed since the mid-1990s. Canada is one of the top five producers of GMO crops in the world. The major GM crops produced in Canada include canola, corn, soy, and, to a lesser extent, sugar beet. Canada also imports GM varieties of cottonseed oil, papaya, and squash, among others. In Canada, GM foods do not require labels advising that the product contains GMOs; any labeling advising of GMO contents is voluntary. According to the International Service for the Acquisition of Agri-Biotech Applications (ISAAA), there were 11.6 million hectares (28.6 million acres) of GM crops grown in Canada in 2012. (Source: *Epoch Times*, July 26, 2013).

Bovine somatotropin (bST) or recombinant bovine growth hormone (rBGH), marketed by Monsanto as Posilac, is a genetically engineered hormone designed to make cows produce more milk. Large amounts of research indicate that bST use has serious implications for the health and welfare of dairy cattle, including making cows more prone to mastitis and sores. Because of evidence that bST milk may cause breast cancer, colon cancer, and prostate cancer in humans, it is banned in Europe. Monsanto has attempted to overturn every ban. As the market leader in GM crops, Monsanto is largely responsible for contaminating the global food chain with GM crops. The long term health effects of eating GM crops are as yet unknown. Resistance to genetically modified foods from the European Union (EU), and many countries, has resulted in a global slowdown of such food.

In 1997, TV journalists Steve Wilson and Jane Akre, who had been making a documentary on the dangers of Monsanto's bST, were fired by their employer *Fox TV. Fox TV* had come under pressure from Monsanto to change the content of the documentary, and when Wilson and Akre refused to be muzzled, they were sacked.

With a sad twist of irony, corporate and government elite dine on safe, organic food, while the masses, those very people who are supposedly represented and protected by their governments, are being poisoned by hidden genetically modified organisms, pesticides, and dangerous contaminants. The former President Barack Obama and his family demanded organic food in their kitchen, yet, behind closed doors, was known to shake hands with the biotech industry.

China's top brass is fed by an exclusive, gated, organic garden, while the rest of the population consumes GM food, steroid contaminated meat, and dairy laced with melamine.

Even Monsanto's own employees command non-genetically modified food in their canteen. Access to clean, organic, and healthy food is not a given right anymore – it has become a political battleground, with the average citizen suffering the loss.

According to Robyn O'Brien, author of *The Unhealthy Truth,* and founder of AllergyKids Foundation, there have been huge increases in the rates of cancer, diabetes, obesity, allergies, and autism. Epidemics have environmental causes, and not genetic ones. According to McKay Jenkins' book, *What's Gotten Into Us?*, some of the greatest threats to our health aren't found in our DNA, but in our food supply and environment.

Summary

Some people have chosen to leave the U.S. due to their distrust of many politicians and some corporations, and to recapture an enjoyable lifestyle. Many have lost their life savings due to the corruption that transpired in the financial industry, which was compounded by a decline in house prices and high unemployment levels in many areas in the U.S.

There has been a decline in the numbers of many species of wildlife, with the main factors for their decline being pesticide use, climate change, and habitat disruption. This chapter provides some of the extent of change and damage that has occurred, and is occurring, to prove my point of the severity of some of the pollution that has taken place on earth by corporations. There are many other examples such as the Exxon Valdez oil spill, and the worst oil spill, which was the Deepwater Horizon, or Gulf of Mexico oil spill.

Although I have cited some major global catastrophic events which have caused significant damage, there are many examples of projects and research which have benefited humanity, namely in the medical, telecommunications and creative industries. Over the past few decades numerous advancements have occurred in other industries.

Mega trends and events to look out for in 2017 include the Donald Trump presidency and what it means for geopolitics, technological disruption and job losses; Brexit and the reshaping of the Euro zone; the movement and price of oil and its impact on oil producers and consumers; and how the world copes with rising terror threats and adverse economic conditions.

Sources: Wikipedia; Corporate Watch; Natural News; Sourcewatch.org; *Monocle; Epoch Times;* Centre for Responsive Politics; *Seeds of Deception* by Jeffrey M. Smith – Chelsea Green Publishing, 2003; The Canadian Encyclopedia; *What's Gotten Into Us?* by McKay Jenkins

ABOUT THE AUTHOR

The author was a designated member of the Appraisal Institute of Canada (AIC) for 40 years from 1974 to 2014. Being a designated member, he was a qualified and respected professional who undertook comprehensive curriculum, experience, and examination requirements to obtain the Accredited Appraiser Canadian Institute (AACI and P.App) designation. He provided unbiased appraisal, review, and consulting assignments on various types of properties in Ontario, Canada. The range of property valuations included hotels, golf courses, schools, a courthouse, a reformatory, a psychiatric hospital, industrial properties, railway corridors, subdivision land, farms, farmland, rural and residential properties and estimating the loss in value due to expropriations.

He was born at the Dr. Antonio Pinto Rosario Hospital on October 16, 1953, in Goa, which was at that time a coastal Portuguese colony on the west coast of India.

The author's father, Cas Castelin, passed away on March 6, 1983. His mother is Clare Rosa Castelin, and his brother is Milton Christopher Castelin.

Although a resident of Toronto, Canada, Mel Castelin has travelled extensively across much of Ontario. His overseas travels included Goa, Florida, California, Mexico, Margarita Island, Costa Rica, Nassau, Cuba, Dominican Republic, Brazil, and Ecuador. His overseas travels have resulted in developing many friendships, and in gaining valuable experience and knowledge.

www.ingramcontent.com/pod-product-compliance
Lightning Source LLC
Chambersburg PA
CBHW050112210326
41519CB00015BA/3937